KEEPING OUR KIDS HOPEFUL

KEEPING OUR KIDS HOPEFUL

PARENTING CHILDREN DURING TIMES OF UNCERTAINTY

DR LYN O'GRADY

Copyright © Lyn O'Grady 2024

All rights reserved. No part of this book may be reproduced or transmitted in any form or by any means, electronic or mechanical, including photocopying, recording or by any information storage and retrieval system, without prior permission in writing from the publisher.

Published by Amba Press
Melbourne, Australia
www.ambapress.com.au

Editor: Andrew Campbell
Cover designer: Tess McCabe

ISBN: 9781923215320 (pbk)
ISBN: 9781923215337 (ebk)

A catalogue record for this book is available from the National Library of Australia.

*For Kleo, our shining light in uncertain times
and why hope-creating matters.*

Contents

About the author		1
Introduction		3
Chapter 1	What is hope?	9
Chapter 2	Positive mental health during childhood	17
Chapter 3	Understanding childhood during the primary school years	29
Chapter 4	Making sense of technology use during childhood	43
Chapter 5	Coping skills for a changing world	55
Chapter 6	Getting along with others	71
Chapter 7	Appreciating attitude – encouraging children to speak up and find their voices	89
Chapter 8	Supporting children through hard times	101
Chapter 9	Recognising and acting on early signs of mental health concerns	113
Chapter 10	Parents caring for themselves	131
Chapter 11	What can parents do to build hope in themselves and their kids?	149
Conclusion		163
Activities and resources		165
References		173
Acknowledgements		177

About the author

Dr Lyn O'Grady is a community psychologist who began her career working with parents in the outer western suburbs of Melbourne in the 1990s. As a young mother herself, she began working with other parents to learn parenting skills. Her interest grew and she began to study psychology, beginning a 16-year journey of studying and working part-time while mothering her two daughters. She continued to focus on working with parents throughout that time as well as moving into schools during the 2000s and then into more strategic project work from 2010. In 2015 she started studying suicidology, completing her master's in 2017, which formed the basis of a book titled *Keeping Our Kids Alive: Parenting a Suicidal Young Person*. In 2019, just before the pandemic struck, she began her own private practice work as a psychologist in Melbourne, and she continues to have a small practice working with clients, supervising psychology interns, and consulting and training.

Introduction

What is it that gets you out of bed every morning? What helps you to face a day when you can't be totally sure what's ahead? What helps you look forward and make plans for the future? It's likely the feeling of hope, a sense of confidence about the future, the belief that our actions will lead us to where we want to be, that we will have a degree of control over what's happening, and that we will be able to cope with what's ahead. Perhaps it's also knowing that we will have people around us who can help if needed. So, what happens when we feel a deep uncertainty about our future lives or recognise that we have very little control over our future? What does this mean for children and how adults support them?

When parents are asked what they want and hope for their children, they typically respond that they want their children to be happy. This makes good sense. Parents don't like to see their children upset or struggling. However, in many ways having happiness as a goal is quite problematic. Firstly, we know that happiness is not a simple idea that is easily achieved just by striving for it. Secondly, focusing on happiness as a goal in itself risks minimising what the child's actual experience might be, leaving a child without the emotional literacy and skills to deal with all of life's experiences, particularly those times when they don't feel happy. It risks teaching a child to silence all those feelings that don't fit with happiness. Thirdly, it is simply impossible for any of us to be happy all the time. If we think about living a rich and fulfilling life, we necessarily will experience a range of emotional experiences which we can choose to embrace and use to understand ourselves. It could be that we learn most about ourselves and the world around us from those experiences that are most uncomfortable and difficult to manage at the time. They are likely to be the experiences that help to define us, reveal what is most important and clarify the way forward.

During the last several decades we have increasingly become aware that children experience their lives in ways that are both similar and different to adults. Children can be more alert and aware of the situations around them than adults realise. They can have strong emotions that are based on a reality that matters to them. They can feel confused and uncertain. In recent years we've started to understand that this is all related to children's mental health. We are better now at recognising that children's behaviour tells us about their inner world and is connected to their mental health. Early childhood settings and schools are now expected to incorporate mental health, wellbeing and/or social and emotional learning programs into their curriculum and to assess children's social and emotional capabilities. We have begun to recognise that individual children can have different needs and ways of seeing the world, with children living with varying abilities and some living with neurodiversity.

Some of these learnings were enhanced during the Covid-19 pandemic. Living and working as a psychologist in Melbourne during our many lockdowns in 2020 and 2021 helped me to reflect on what we might take for granted and what we all need to live in a way that is satisfying and enjoyable. That time gave us an opportunity to gain an appreciation of how the way we live our lives, spend time, and connect with each other affects how we feel about ourselves and cope with our day-to-day life. With our schools and community venues closed and visits to family and friends restricted, we needed to focus more inwardly, beginning to question what it means to live a satisfying life. We also understood the need to do this for the good of others, for the community. We initially had a sense of "being in it together". We recognised the unusual phenomenon that the pandemic was and could see ourselves as people living through a period of history that would be significant, even if we didn't fully understand what it meant at the time. Over time our understandings and tolerance shifted as the difficulties worsened. We started to see that some of us were more deeply impacted than others. Parents had to make sense of the experience for themselves as well as for their children. As adults, we can have a sense of perspective that places this kind of unique experience in context – it's highly unusual, it's a period of time rather than being forever, and it's something we can best get through by supporting each other. Children on the other hand could not possibly have that kind of perspective. The younger the child, the larger the proportion of their lives the pandemic took up, making it harder to envision a sense of future. Their day-to-day experiences, where they learn about the world around them through living in the here and now to develop their social and emotional skills with others, were restricted.

Over time, the impact of the pandemic on children began to be seen, and we are continuing to see the impact of the lockdowns and that time of uncertainty on children's development, family relationships, and the capacity of schools to cope. While there was some recognition that time spent at home without the pressures of a busy lifestyle had some benefits, there was also a lot of concern about children missing out on education, pressures on parents to support children to learn at home and, especially, children's lack of opportunities for social engagement. The pandemic highlighted what a child needs to grow and learn well. We also started to see how families benefit from having supports around them and sharing the responsibility of raising a child. We may have known much of this already, but the experience of the pandemic helped us to home in on what was most important, in a way that is difficult when life is busy with many competing demands. Taking time to stop and reflect when faced with a challenge can help us to see through the fog of the daily tasks of our lives and pinpoint what is most important.

It's appealing to think about childhood as an idyllic time that's carefree and happy, with no responsibilities – a time to have fun before the stresses of adolescence and adulthood fall on us. In recent years, however, this protective bubble has begun to burst and we've started to understand that children can also experience mental health difficulties. Many adults describe their own childhoods as less than idyllic, but there's often been a silence around this kind of experience. This new awareness, and willingness to see what is really happening for children, has led to a focus on mental health support in schools and information to help parents recognise the signs of an emerging mental health problem.

This newfound awareness around mental health concerns in children is useful, but if, as often happens with new knowledge, the pendulum swings towards a focus on mental illness, we may miss the opportunity to focus on positive mental health – what it is that helps children to develop and thrive. Trying to understand mental health in the same way as physical health has led to some confusion and misinformation. Our physical and mental health are linked, but our mental health is in many ways less visible than physical health. There are no x-rays or blood tests to diagnose mental health problems. We certainly need to recognise the signs of mental health problems, assess and diagnose them and then have effective treatments that include the child within the context of their family, school and community. However, if our only discourse about mental health is in the context of problems and illness, we are not prioritising all the ways we can understand and promote positive mental health. These opportunities occur for children, families, schools and communities every day, in every interaction, in every attempt at doing something new or different, in every achievement – and of course in every challenge. If we start to see the ways that both achievements and challenges can help build positive mental health, we can start to help children's self-awareness and self-knowledge develop early on and continue to build over time. This not only makes their childhood more enjoyable but also sets them up well for adolescence and even adulthood. We've known since the days of Freud that those early years of life are significant and can set the path for future life. Knowing how to feel confident and enjoy life is perhaps the foundation of being able to remain hopeful.

In my work with children and parents as a psychologist, I aim to help parents to get to know their children better, to listen and work towards understanding them, as they continue to develop, to be warm and caring but also confident to provide guidance and place limits on their behaviour when required. Children benefit from an authoritative parenting style where rules are explained, they know what is going on, and they are encouraged to make decisions as much as is developmentally appropriate at any point in time. This helps children feel confident and capable of making their own decisions when not with their parents. If they feel they have a voice in the family, they will grow up better understanding how to speak up and ask for help. If parents help children to understand themselves through everyday opportunities, children will become more literate in mental health concepts and able to apply them more independently over time. The way parenting occurs is particularly important during times of uncertainty and stress. The impact of parenting experiences echoes well into the future.

In my work with adults, I am often aware that I'm actually witnessing and helping the person deal with the outcomes of parenting styles where they, as children, were not heard or respected. In those situations, children didn't have a voice and were not provided with support to understand themselves. This leaves their adult selves confused about who they are and often overwhelmed when trying to negotiate an enduring relationship with their parents (and others). It's hard to remain hopeful when feeling so overwhelmed over a long period of time. It's hard also to watch people struggling to find hope or reluctant to trust that being hopeful won't harm them. Perhaps the art of turning up for help is a significant act towards hope.

I'm aware of the responsibility I feel in helping people to find ways to have hope that is realistic and fosters a desire to keep trying.

These experiences have consolidated my view about the importance of parents being supported to understand their children's development and more able to create environments where children have a voice and can be supported to express their feelings safely and with growing confidence. This will go a long way towards instilling a sense of hope and possibility for children into the future.

CHAPTER 1

What is hope?

When thinking about our lives after the Covid-19 pandemic in an increasingly complex and uncertain world, I began to think about how challenging it can be to remain hopeful about our lives now and into the future. I see this sometimes when working with people who find their lives overwhelming and are unable to envisage a positive future. I wrote my book *Keeping Our Kids Alive: Parenting a Suicidal Young Person* because I was aware of the way that a lack of hope can infiltrate young people's thinking and lead to thoughts of dying and acts of harm to themselves, and how difficult it could be for parents to know what to do. In my work and discussions with others since then, I've recognised that this lack of hope often doesn't just happen in adolescence, but its seeds can begin earlier, during childhood, though the despair may not grow or become obvious to others until the adolescent years. The instilling of hope in children has therefore become a new priority for me.

While current world challenges – such as climate change, the demands of technology in our lives, information overload, economic pressures, images of wars flowing into our screens, and disconnect between community members – are many, humans have capacity to respond to challenges through adapting and being there for each other. We saw this during the pandemic and, if we look, we see everyday acts of care and kindness that help us feel connected and supported within families and communities. Interestingly, American writer Rebecca Solnit describes this not knowing what is going to happen, or how, or when, and that very uncertainty as the "space of hope" (2016, p. xxi).

Understanding hope

In seeking out ways to understand this relationship between uncertainty and hope, I came across the School of Life's *Reasons to be Hopeful*. In using art works to explore ideas related to despair and hope, they conclude:

> *the only honest position is to face the future with radical open-mindedness. We can't and don't know what is coming. Therefore, a primary reason to carry on is the hope of eventually stumbling on further, unexpected reasons to be hopeful. We must banish our despairing surety about what is ahead – the future version of ourselves may look back on who we are right now and beseech us to keep faith with the journey. We can't know about the years to come, and for that reason alone, we must give ourselves every generous chance to find out. There will be plenty more reasons to be hopeful; our list is only just starting (2023, p. 221).*

As parents, developing this radical open-mindedness may be the best way to live our lives, while also providing that model for our children. Being uncertain about the future, according to that idea, doesn't have to be negative. It can be reframed as a positive way to approach a future that is not, and perhaps cannot be, known. Learning to be open-minded may come naturally to us, or not. It perhaps requires a positivity and curiosity that we can develop. It fits well with how we can think about hope.

Rebecca Solnit similarly brings a positive view to uncertainty when she says "[h]ope locates itself in the premises that we don't know what will happen and that in the spaciousness of uncertainty is room to act" (2016, p. xii). She expands on this by saying that "[w]hen you recognise uncertainty, you recognise that you may be able to influence the outcomes – you alone or you in concert with a few dozen or several million others" (2016, p. xii). In this way, she draws in the way that optimism and pessimism relate to hope:

> *Hope is the embrace of the unknown and unknowable, an alternative to the certainty of both optimists and pessimists. Optimists think it will all be fine without our involvement; pessimists take the opposite position; both excuse themselves from action. It's the belief that what we do matters even though how and when it may matter, who and what it may impact, are not things we can know beforehand (2016, p. xii).*

Solnit impresses me with her ability to embrace hope as a way to live life well within a context of uncertainty by facing the challenges we encounter. As adults supporting children, this message seems like an important one to me.

Conditions for hope

Understanding hope as a way of thinking, or a cognitive process, involves three main conditions:

1. **Goals** – having something to hope for. Goals can be anything we desire to get, to be, to experience, or to create. Ideally, they are personally meaningful and provide a sense of purpose. Having goals that are connected to our most important personal values will be most motivating and lead to greater wellbeing than goals that don't fit well with our values. Values are the beliefs and principles that are important in the way we live. They help guide our decisions and the way we act towards others.

2. **Pathways** – the ability to find ways to achieve goals or to overcome obstacles. These can be complex but can also begin with anything that will contribute positively to achieving whatever goal is being embraced. It can help to establish a

set of small steps that can be tackled one at a time to avoid becoming overwhelmed by a goal that seems unachievable. Being prepared to face obstacles and discover new goals as you learn about yourself will help you to adjust the pathway to remain motivated.

3. **Agency** – the motivation that pushes us to strive for our goals. This comes from our beliefs about ourselves. Sometimes negative beliefs about our abilities can get in the way of remaining hopeful. Becoming aware of the messages we send ourselves that are unhelpful ("I can't do this", "I won't be able to", "I'm not good enough") is a good first step to recognising one of the barriers to having agency, replacing these thoughts with more positive self-talk ("I might be able to do this" or "I could give it a try") (Snyder, et al., 2002).

Adopting these optimistic and self-confident approaches to solving problems is likely to reduce the negative effects of hopelessness and build wellbeing and psychological resilience. In the field of positive psychology, building on the work of Martin Seligman, the concept of hope is frequently included in research and found to not only promote positive psychological outcomes but also reduce many negative psychological outcomes, such as anxiety, depressive symptoms, and suicidal ideation.

Different types of hope

Hope is not just one thing. There are different types of hope:

1. **Realistic hope** – hope for an outcome that is reasonable or probable. This type of hope allows people to observe and understand their situation while also maintaining openness towards the possibility of positive change. Setting small goals might make this achievable.
2. **Utopian hope** – a collectively oriented hope that collaborative action can lead to a better future for all. This involves rejecting the present and being driven by hope to affirm a

better alternative. This might be present in political or social movements where people come together to expand the horizons of possibility.

3. **Chosen hope** – hope that manages despair and challenges associated with an uncertain future or situations that can be difficult to change. This might be the case when a person has a serious or terminal illness, for example, but feels hopeful towards goals within the limits of the situation.

4. **Transcendent or existential hope** – a stance of general hopefulness not tied to a specific outcome or goal, such as the hope that something good will happen. This can include patient hope (that everything will work out well in the end); generalised hope (not directed towards a specific outcome); and universal hope (a general belief in the future and a defence against despair in the face of challenges).

While hope can be a helpful approach to life, having false hope can be unhelpful and lead to poor decision-making or a sense of failure. This can occur if hopes were based on possibilities rather than what is probable and able to be planned for. Ensuring that hope is based on planned goals that are realistic can therefore be helpful. Recognising the benefits of support can also help improve the imagining of positive possibilities as well as the ability to achieve goals. As parents, modelling ways of seeing the world through a hopeful lens, engaging with the world in a curious way, and looking to connect with others might be the most useful ways to promote hope in children. This necessarily means also coping with the many demands and pressures faced when living with children and helping them develop across their various stages and ages.

The School of Life (2023) explains that there can be times when we don't really question our existence or the role that hope may play. There may then be other times when our moods shift and aspects of our lives become more doubtful or painful. It may be difficult to do things like getting up in the morning with purpose, or we may "go through the motions, but our spirit is elsewhere" (p. 7). At those times our society might apply labels such as depression. As I see in my work as a psychologist, there is an intrinsic link between being hopeful and having positive mental health. I am most concerned about my clients (both children and adults) when I see their sense of hope and possibility fading. At those times I try to help them reconnect with positive experiences from their past and the unique values and beliefs that make them who they are. Importantly, I try to help them connect with others who know them and see them as the unique individuals they are. For children, this necessarily includes those people closest to them – their parents and carers, extended family members, and teachers. Parents in turn need to do this for themselves by connecting with others so they are able to connect with their children throughout everyone's daily joys and struggles.

REFLECTIVE QUESTIONS

- What helps you to feel hopeful?
- When in your life were you most hopeful?
- When has hope helped you get through a challenging time?
- What stories fill you with hope?
- How do you talk with your children about hope?
- What hopeful stories can you share with your children?
- How do you demonstrate hope in your day-to-day life?
- What stops you from feeling hopeful?
- Who supports you in being hopeful?
- When does it seem that hope isn't enough?

CHAPTER 2

Positive mental health during childhood

Mental health can be an aspect of ourselves that we don't tend to think about until something goes wrong. Unlike our physical health, our mental health can be invisible. It might show itself in the way we think and in our behaviours. This is particularly the case for children, with the risk that this can lead to a focus on the behaviour rather than what might actually be underlying the behaviour. Mental and physical health are connected, so basic needs such as sleeping, eating and exercise are closely related to our mental health. This can add to the confusion about what mental health is. The risk of focusing on our mental health mostly when it becomes a problem means that we tend to think of mental health problems or mental illness rather than positive mental health. We tend to think less about what we can do to help ourselves to feel good mentally. That means by the time we are thinking about our mental health we are already a few steps behind and problems might already be arising. So what do we mean by mental health? What does mental health mean for children? How can we focus on positive aspects of mental health?

How can we understand children's mental health?

The World Health Organisation helps us to see how our mental health relates to all aspects of our lives. In relation to children, the World Health Organisation states that:

> *childhood and adolescence are critical stages of life for mental health and wellbeing. This is when young people develop skills in self-control, social interaction and learning. Negative experiences – at home due to family conflict or at school due to bullying, for example – have a damaging effect on the development of these core cognitive and emotional skills (2023).*

This suggests that we need to create opportunities for children to learn and have positive experiences as well as prevent negative experiences where possible or support children when negative experiences do arise (because they can sometimes be difficult to prevent). Understanding the effects of conflict and bullying can lead us to work towards preventing them in the future and also to provide support to help children recover from the impact. Keeping children safe physically and emotionally needs to be a basic starting point for children's mental health. When we think about children's mental health, it helps to think about their stage of development, their physical health and abilities, their connections with family members (including extended family) and friends, their engagement in learning environments, and opportunities they have to play. We can see them as individuals (with their own strengths, limitations and unique personality) while also as part of our family and broader community. It helps to prioritise what they need in the moment but also have the end goal of helping them to develop the skills they will need for the future.

When I returned to working directly with children as a psychologist in late 2019 after a break of 10 years working on projects, I noticed some big changes in the way children engaged in play. The effects of technology were evident and I've had to work hard to help children take an interest in the farm set, doll's house and games that I offered them in my office. Some children even asked where the devices were. I didn't know at that time that another major life event was about to arise that would significantly affect children and their families. Covid-19 arrived with its lockdowns and my work took on a different focus as we all adjusted to staying at home more. For children, this meant more time at home with family (which had positive effects for some who enjoyed the additional time with parents and siblings but also very negative effects for others when family conflict and abuse increased). Children's engagement with schools necessarily changed as they began to learn at home instead of turning up at school every morning. It quickly became clear that some families were better equipped to manage that than others. School staff worked with parents to do their very best in the circumstances. Understanding how children's mental health is impacted by the world around them, it then makes sense that children's mental health changed during the period that followed – some did well and their mental health improved, while many others struggled. We are still learning about the full impact on children of this period of time and we are very likely to continue to see the aftermath of the lockdowns and changes in children's lives for some time.

A continuum of wellbeing

In the National Children's Mental Health and Wellbeing Strategy released by the Australian Government in 2021 it is noted that:

> *The mental health and wellbeing of children defines their childhood experience and impacts their ability to live a long and contributing life... Good mental health and wellbeing enables children to reach their full potential, experience fulfilling relationships, and adapt and cope with challenging circumstances (National Mental Health Commission, 2021, p. 4).*

The strategy uses a wellbeing continuum (overleaf) to capture how mental health can change.

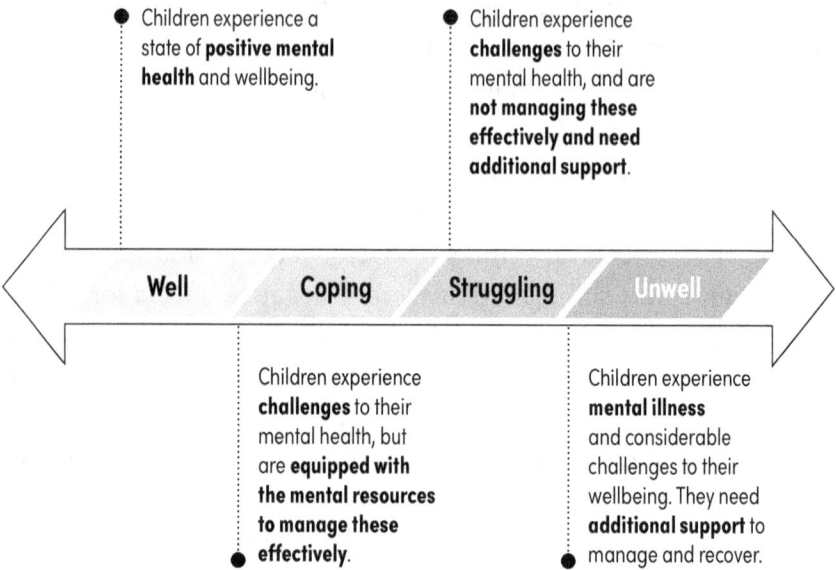

It is useful to note that most children in Australia are doing well with their mental health. Some children will be starting to show signs of mental health difficulties, and the earlier we can notice and act on those signs the more able we will be to help them move back towards wellness. Even when children are struggling or have a diagnosable mental health problem, we can still work on ways to improve their overall wellbeing and ensure that they, and their families, receive help to continue to grow and develop.

What does a mentally healthy child look like?

It can help us to reflect on what a mentally healthy child looks like. We might think that a mentally healthy child is happy and not bothered by life. This in some ways reflects an idyllic view of childhood that is mostly unrealistic (and perhaps connected to our desire for children to be happy). While children's lives can be supported and buffered by support from the adults around them, the reality is that even the most well-supported child will experience some challenges and struggles. In fact, part of being mentally healthy is being able to deal with those challenges by facing them, seeking support as necessary, and working one's way through the problem. When children are so protected that they don't get the opportunity to feel the emotions that come with difficulties or get involved in problem-solving, their mental health won't be supported, and over time they will become less capable of resolving problems for themselves. This in turn could lead to mental health problems. We might understand this ability to cope as resilience – where children are faced with some kind of upset or adversity and are supported to deal with it so they can feel good about themselves and learn how to deal with similar problems in the future. Often resilience is misunderstood as the need for children to toughen up, not be affected by experiences, and get on with life. That approach to understanding resilience is unhelpful and potentially damaging, as it is dismissive of the experiences of children and the role that support plays in resilience.

Children bring their own personalities and temperaments to the situations they face. Combine this with the personalities and temperaments of parents, other family members, teachers and other adults they come into contact with, and we have a recipe for complexity. As adults, the way we respond to others is determined by the way we see the world, our own life experiences (particularly during our childhood), and what we have learned (and our willingness to keep learning) along the way. In this way family members play a critical role in the lives of children. Parents therefore need to look after their own mental health and wellbeing to be able to care for their children. They also need to be able to adjust to the changing needs of children as they grow and if they have more than one child to meet the different needs of each child, each with their own stage of development and personality.

We know that the relationships between parents and other family members and the child are critical to the child feeling safe and supported. We call this attachment and we've known about it now for decades. We know that it begins from birth and continues to develop throughout our lives, even into adulthood as we build new relationships. Our attachment style develops as a result of these connections and will affect how we relate to others throughout our lives. Being present and spending time with children, tuning in to their feelings and needs while also respecting their individuality, are all important ways to build and maintain what we call secure attachment during childhood. Secure attachment allows children to feel comfortable within themselves and able to connect with others in healthy ways.

A child with positive mental health will experience changes in moods and sometimes experience difficulties in managing situations they face. They may sometimes behave in ways that we don't like. At times they might surprise us with what they know and at other times they may surprise us with what they haven't understood or remembered. Childhood is a time of learning and being exposed to a range of situations that help children to understand how the world works, where they fit in it, and how they will respond. This requires them to be exposed to a lot of different experiences, given the opportunity to respond in their own way as well as being guided and supported towards responding in ways that are helpful and safe to themselves and others. What this looks like will change depending on the age and stage of development of the child. What we expect of a five-year-old will be different to what we expect of an eight-year-old or a 10-year-old, yet at times it may seem that our 10-year-old is behaving like a two-year-old (or conversely like a 15-year-old). When we understand these stages of development as helpful and necessary for the child to learn about themselves and their world, we will be more able to adjust our own expectations and levels of tolerance to continue to engage with them in helpful ways. Children with a disability or who are neurodiverse may not see the world as we expect them to or be able to respond in ways that are age appropriate. This can lead to distress in us and we can then react in a way that's unhelpful and potentially shaming of the child. If we, on the other hand, see these behaviours as signs of the child being challenged or overwhelmed by a situation and needing some extra support, we can feel more confident and able to respond in a way that is more positive and helpful. This is the kind of approach that will support a child's mental health. Accepting children as they are while helping them to adjust their behaviours to the situation is critical in promoting mental health and helping children develop.

One of the key ways that we can understand and support mental health is to understand feelings. Feelings are like our guide to tell us what is happening to us, what is important to us, and to alert us that something is OK or could be a problem. By understanding and knowing how to respond to our feelings, we are better able to learn about ourselves. This takes time and in many ways is a lifelong task as we continue to face new situations and experiences. This learning begins in childhood as we watch those around us, particularly parents and other adults we spend time with, deal with their emotions. Our emotions are closely related to our thoughts and values. This in turn flows into the way we respond or behave in any particular situation.

Social and emotional learning skills as a basis for positive mental health

A useful way to think about learning about emotions, based on the work of the Collaborative for Academic, Social, and Emotional Learning (www.casel.org) is to think about these different areas:

- **Self-awareness** – recognising and naming our own emotions, thoughts and values and understanding how they influence behaviour in different contexts. This includes recognising strengths and limitations while also having a sense of confidence and purpose.
- **Self-management** – managing our emotions, thoughts and behaviours effectively in different situations. This includes the ability to delay gratification, cope with stress, and feel motivation and agency to accomplish personal and collective goals.

- **Social awareness** – understanding the perspective of others and being able to empathise with them, including those from different backgrounds and in different contexts. This includes being able to feel compassion for others, understand broader historical and social norms for behaviour in different settings, and recognise family, school and community resources and supports.
- **Relationship skills** – the ability to establish and maintain healthy and supportive relationships and to effectively navigate settings with a range of different individuals and groups. This includes being able to communicate clearly, listen actively, co-operate, work collaboratively to problem-solve and resolve conflict constructively, navigate settings with differing social and cultural demands and opportunities, provide leadership, and seek or offer help when needed.
- **Responsible decision-making** – the ability to make caring and constructive choices about personal behaviour and social interactions across different situations. This includes ethical standards and safety concerns, and evaluating the benefits and consequences of various actions for personal, social and collective wellbeing.

As you look at this list of abilities, you'll notice that they are quite complex skills, especially for children. It's useful to remember that children learn these skills gradually in line with their stage of development. We know that children follow patterns and order in their development (e.g., think of your child learning to walk – they may crawl, then begin to stand and hold onto furniture, stand briefly before falling down, take steps with support, and finally be able to co-ordinate themselves to begin to walk), but there are also individual differences, with children progressing at their own rate. There is not an absolutely "normal" way for children to develop, although there are milestones that we need to look out for as a guide. Children can also sometimes regress during times of stress and change. Children's social and emotional learning occurs through watching people around them and importantly through explicitly being taught and having opportunities to practise. We know that they need the explicit teaching and practice in order to fully understand and be able to develop competency. Watching others is useful and will be influential but is not sufficient for all children to learn these skills and become confident in the various situations they will find themselves in. Children who are neurodiverse will need additional support, practice and repetition to learn these skills, but it's important to know that there are ways that all children can learn these skills over time. Research is clear that the benefits of children learning social and emotional skills include better academic performance, improved attitudes and behaviours, less negative behaviours, and reduced emotional stress (Durlak et al., 2022).

You may feel uncertain about using emotions to help your child learn about themselves and others. You might consider these skills as "soft" or less relevant than practical skills or developing an ability to get on and not be affected by feelings. Perhaps this is an area that you didn't learn about as a child, or now don't feel very comfortable or confident in. It can help to remember that this is lifelong learning and we all continue to learn these skills. It's never too late, and helping children to learn them can be a real incentive to encourage ourselves to learn about them too.

Parents working on their own mental health and wellbeing

In his book *Permission to Feel: Unlocking the Power of Emotions to Achieve Wellbeing and Success* (2019), Marc Brackett, a professor from Yale University, outlines seven strategies to help parents:

1. **Permission to feel** – are you an emotion scientist (curious) or an emotion judge (critical)? What's your self-efficacy around emotion regulation – how confident do you feel about managing emotions?

2. **Managing your physiology** – mindful breathing and meditation.
3. **Managing your body's budget** – sleep, nutrition and exercise.
4. **Managing your thoughts** – positive self-talk, re-appraisal, visualisation and gratitude.
5. **Managing relationships** – being around people who help you to feel safe, heard and connected (co-regulated).
6. **Managing situations** – modifying and selecting situations to prevent stress, having routines.
7. **Finding purpose/meaning/fun** – spirituality or religion; hobbies/leisure activity, entertainment, experiencing nature.

Hopefully by now you can see how positive mental health has some key elements, with the bottom line being physical health and basic needs of safety being met, then the development of skills and behaviours that relate to our emotions and thoughts, all within a context of what makes life meaningful for us. As parents, a useful starting point will be to explore this for ourselves, by reflecting on the way we look after ourselves and are continuing to learn about our emotions and thoughts. Of course, one of the best ways to continue to learn and consolidate our learning is to teach someone else, and you have a perfect candidate in your child who is just waiting to learn all about it. Perhaps you will also now better see how the Covid-19 lockdowns may have had such an impact on children's development as opportunities to learn and practise these social and emotional skills were limited.

If you find this particularly challenging and become concerned about your child's mental health, you can reach out to your child's school or your family's general practitioner to discuss your concerns. This is all part of the help-seeking behaviour that is important to model to children. We also know that intervening as early as possible is helpful in identifying any concerns and ensuring that any support or interventions can be put into place quickly.

REFLECTIVE QUESTIONS

- How would you describe mental health in your own words?
- Does your child talk about any school activities that help them learn about mental health?
- What have you found most useful about thinking about positive mental health in children?
- What surprised you?
- What would you like to know more about?
- How does thinking about positive mental health help you think about your child's behaviour and needs differently?
- In what ways do you support your own positive mental health?
- What have you noticed about your child as you read this chapter?
- How do you feel about using emotions to help your child learn about themselves and others?

CHAPTER 3

Understanding childhood during the primary school years

We can consider the primary school years as a relatively calm period, as children's growth and development occur at a slower rate than they do during early childhood or during puberty and the adolescent years to come. That's not to say that there's no change happening or that it's smooth sailing for all children. In fact, these are the years when children become more aware of the world around them as they start to connect with other children and adults from outside of the family.

When I was six years old I began to develop what I now understand to be an anxiety problem. We'd moved towns with my dad's job a few months after I started school, so after some initial school reluctance because of my shyness when I first began school, I'd had to settle into my second school in a small space of time. I have a vague recollection of sitting in the classroom and feeling the urge to go to the bathroom – often. After some time, this must have led to the teacher raising her concern with my mum, who took me to the family doctor. Quite quickly, I think, I was hospitalised, and my parents were advised that my kidneys were failing. I, of course, had no idea about this but recall spending time in the hospital bed in a shared room with a boy whom I found very annoying. He was noisy and running around all the time. I, on the other hand, was a compliant patient and stayed in bed, probably feeling quite bewildered by the whole experience. The nurses offered me comics, which I rejected, so they arranged for my teacher to send me some "real" books to read. I can remember feeling very lonely and isolated away from my parents and siblings and recall the comfort the books provided me.

Thankfully, it turned out that my kidneys weren't actually failing and after a few days I was allowed to return home. The doctor told my parents to just put me in a room with books and leave me to it. My lifelong love of books was born (or was it there already and then simply amplified?). My mum, no doubt relieved by this news, set out to follow the doctor's advice and implement this solution. She would leave me at the local bookshop while she shopped for the family's fortnightly groceries. My parents paid the exorbitant amount that sets of encyclopaedias cost in those days so I had a ready supply of reading material. Even now, I continue to turn to reading and the comfort of books on a very regular basis and have a house filled with books, most of which I will never be able to read. I now know there's a name for this: the Japanese word *tsundoku*, which means acquiring reading materials but letting them pile up in one's home without reading them!

There's much to learn from this childhood experience, and I often find myself reflecting back on that time when I think about my own responses now as a much older adult – how it may have been an early trigger for my interest in psychology broadly and choosing to work with children and parents more specifically. The situation arose at a time when children were still largely seen and not heard, when expectations (particularly of an older child in a family of three children) were high in relation to appropriate ways to behave, and there wasn't really much of a language for feelings. My parents provided me with a safe and secure environment, yet I'd been through quite a lot of change in that short timeframe. My personality meant that I would be quiet and compliant rather than loud and outspoken. It's no wonder, then, that my anxious feelings showed themselves through physical signs. This led us on a necessary medical pathway to look for, and ultimately rule out, underlying physical causes. Recognising my interest in books and using this to focus my attention and provide comfort was a pretty helpful solution. Learning the skills to identify and manage feelings, particularly worries, was still required, but at least I had an outlet. This was no doubt the case for most children at that time, but I managed to work it out for myself and then over time to learn and adjust to future changes and challenges – learning that continues today. It's no wonder that I'm now very interested in creating a world where we understand children better and can prevent mental health issues.

Helping children to develop their own ideas

One of the most important ways to support children is to give them a legitimate voice to share their ideas. This requires us to listen to what they are thinking or worrying about. That's why I like the climate change strikes and activities that children are so active in. I love seeing children having opportunities to be themselves and engage in the world in ways that adults might not have thought about. At the same time, I'm constantly aware of the need to help children (and their parents) to create a balance in their lives about what they know and are concerned about, having ways to manage those situations and also to keep having fun as they learn about the world around them. I love seeing children come up with their own solutions for problems that arise, whether it's drawing a picture to have beside their bed to scare away their nightmares, creating an image of their family to take on camp, or developing their own feelings cards to help them recognise and manage their strong feelings. It's always clear to me that children's own ideas for solving problems are the best, but also we need to be ready to provide additional ideas or guidance. Listening first and letting children gain confidence in their own abilities is the best starting point for any problem. Otherwise we risk disempowering the child or creating a solution for a problem that isn't actually the problem at hand. In this way, we can see one role of parents as coaching children to develop their abilities to create and think independently. We have to be careful not to fall into the trap of thinking we always know better just because we are adults.

If you reflect back over the years, you will be aware of all of the developmental changes your child has been through. Many of the changes in early childhood were visible and happened quite quickly. During the primary school years our children go through considerable changes but at a slower rate. Some of these changes are physical, like their height and appearance, but many of them are less obvious and can happen in spurts. This development occurs within the context of living in the family, possibly with extended family members, the local community and school. Each of these influences or settings can play a role in the way that a child develops. The broader society, including policies and societal expectations, also affects the way children interact with others and their environment. We just need to remember the impact of mandated lockdowns during the Covid-19 pandemic to recognise how this works.

Human development stages during childhood

Childhood is the period of physical, cognitive and social growth that begins at birth and continues through to adolescence. There are five main areas of human development that occur during this time:

- **Physical development** – changes in size, shape and physical maturity of the body, including physical abilities and co-ordination.
- **Intellectual/cognitive development** – the learning and use of language, the ability to reason, problem-solve and organise ideas. This is related to brain development.

- **Social development** – the process of gaining the knowledge and skills needed to interact successfully with others.
- **Emotional development** – feelings and emotional responses to events, changes in understanding one's own feelings, and appropriate forms of expressing them.
- **Moral development** – the growing understanding of right and wrong, and the changes in behaviour caused by that understanding, sometimes called a conscience.

The primary school period (five to 12 years of age) can be considered middle childhood and has been described as a crucial yet underappreciated phase of human development, because

on the surface it can appear like a slow-motion interlude between the spectacular transformations of infancy and early childhood and those of adolescence. In reality, this life stage is anything but static: the transition from early to middle childhood heralds a global shift in cognition, motivation, and social behavior, with profound and wide-ranging implications for the development of personality, sex differences and even psychopathology (DelGiudice, 2018, p. 95).

Development in middle childhood

Physical changes	- Mid-growth spurt, followed by decelerating skeletal growth - Increased muscle mass - Increased Body Mass Index - Initial development of axillary hair and body odour - Increased sex difference, bone strength and muscularity - Emergence of sex differences in vocal characteristics
Brain growth	- Approaching peak of overall brain volume - Peak of grey matter volume - Continuing increase in white matter volume/integrity

Motor and perceptual skills	- Increased gross motor skills (e.g., walking)
- Increased fine motor skills (e.g., handwriting)
- Local-global shift in visual processing preferences
- Increased self-regulation and executive functions (inhibition, attention, planning, etc.)
- Increased mentalising skills (multiple perspectives, conflicting goals)
- Increased navigational skills (working memory, ability to understand maps)
- Complex moral reasoning (conflicting points of view)
- Increased pragmatic abilities (gossiping, storytelling, verbal competition, etc.)
- Consolidation of status/dominance hierarchies)
- Changes in aggression levels (individual trajectories)
- Development of disgust
- Changes in food preferences (e.g., spicy foods)
- Onset of sexual/romantic attraction
- Increased frequency of sexual play
- Increased sense of gender identity
- Peak of sex segregation
- Peak of sex differences in social play (including play fighting vs play parenting)
- Increased sex differences in physical aggression (males greater than females)
- Emergence of sex differences in attachment styles
Psychopathology	- Early peak of psychopathology onset (externalising, anxiety, phobias, ADHD)
- Peak onset of fetishistic attractions
- Emergence of sex differences in conduct disorders (males more than females)
Social context	- Active involvement in caretaking, foraging, domestic tasks, helping
- Expectations of responsible behaviour
- Attribution of individuality and personhood ("getting noticed")

Behaviour genetics	• Increased heritability of general intelligence and language skills • New genetic influences on general intelligence, language, aggression, and prosociality

SOURCE: DELGIUDICE (2018)

As indicated in the table above, the most dramatic changes occur in the areas of self-regulation and executive functions as children become much more capable of inhibiting unwanted behaviour, maintaining sustained attention, making and following plans, and so forth. Parallel improvements occur in the ability to understand and represent mental states (known as mentalising) and moral reasoning, as children become more able to consider multiple perspectives and conflicting goals.

The role of social development during childhood

The life stage of middle childhood has two major interlocking functions:

1. Social learning, and
2. Social integration in a system of roles, norms, activities and shared knowledge.

While children are still receiving sustained investment from parents and other family members in the form of food, protection, knowledge, etc., they also start to actively contribute to their family's functioning. It's important then for parents to provide opportunities for children to participate in family life. Children develop these skills by having the skills modelled to them, being explicitly taught, and then practising, with support and feedback as needed. Some children will willingly seek out opportunities to join in and will help when asked, while others might be more internally focused and less willing to participate in chores or household tasks. Finding ways to navigate both of these situations is an important consideration for parents. Having one child taking on too much responsibility can become just as problematic as a child who does nothing to contribute to the family's functioning.

There are various ways this can be tackled in a family. Family meetings can be quite a formal way to approach it, where the value of helping each other to get things done can be discussed with a list of chores for sharing. Having a way to record this will be helpful. Tailoring the chores to the age and interests of the child is likely to make it more successful. Having a reward system might be useful to begin with as a motivator, but there are a couple of problems with rewards – they don't work after a short period of time and they are an external motivator. Ideally, children will learn the value of doing jobs because helping each other helps us feel good. Other families might take a less formal approach and create an environment where everyone pitches in to help when asked or when it's obvious that others need help. Letting children know the tasks, helping them learn how to do them, and thanking them for their efforts are really important in building success. Adjusting as children grow and including them in plans for how the tasks will be done will be helpful. Including children in these tasks can be a way to make them feel valued and part of the family and help them develop skills that can transfer to other settings where being helpful and caring about others is valued.

Childhood as a life stage

Another model for understanding child development is based on the work of Erik Erikson, an American-German psychologist (1902–1994). He developed eight stages of development, the first four of which relate to childhood:

1. **Infancy – trust vs mistrust.** Infants depend on caregivers for basic needs such as food. Infants learn to trust others based on how well caregivers meet their needs. As caregivers fill an infant's needs, the baby develops a sense of trust and security.

2. **Toddlerhood – autonomy vs shame and self-doubt.** During this phase, young children begin exploring the world around them to learn about the environment and their place in it. Caregivers serve as a safe base from which the child can explore the world. When caregivers encourage independence, children will feel secure enough to take risks. When children are discouraged, they may develop feelings of shame. If caregivers foster excessive dependence, the child may learn to doubt their own abilities.
3. **Preschool years – initiative vs guilt.** Preschoolers are increasingly focused on doing things for themselves and establishing their own goals. When caregivers nurture these tendencies, children learn how to make decisions. If children are criticised for being assertive, they may feel guilty for pursuing their desires.
4. **Early school years – industry vs inferiority.** As children grow in independence, they become increasingly aware of themselves as individuals and begin to compare themselves with others. Children who are accomplished compared to their peers can develop self-confidence and pride. Children who do not achieve milestones may doubt their abilities or self-worth. When children are constantly criticised, they may develop feelings of inferiority.

The work of Erikson highlights the critical role of caregivers in children's development. It is through the day-to-day perspectives and behaviours of parents in their modelling and interactions with children that children learn about themselves and others, which underpins their development. All of the developmental changes (social, cognitive, emotional and physical) interact with the others and come together to create the uniqueness of each child.

The emergence of puberty

Puberty often occurs earlier than parents expect and can sometimes catch parents by surprise. Well before the physical changes of puberty there will be hormonal changes which trigger those changes. Both visible and hidden changes can affect all aspects of the child's body and mind: their sense of who they are, their place in the family and society, their assumptions about the world around them, their capacity to do things (and perceptions about what they can do), and their relationships with family members, peers and teachers. This can begin what may well become a lifelong questioning, shaped variously by relationships with others across the course of the lifespan. With puberty, children are moving rapidly towards the "work" of adolescence to test boundaries and explore how new things can lay the path for the development of their future selves. This in-between phase can be challenging for parents, who need to manage their child's changing behaviours and attitudes while continuing to offer support and guidance given the child's age. This is no mean feat, and the challenges it presents can be underestimated as we typically hear more about the challenges of adolescence itself than this period of pre-adolescence.

It is now recognised that the changes associated with puberty are actually occurring much earlier than in the past. Researchers have measured puberty since the 1940s, when key aspects of adolescent development, including socio-emotional, cognitive and behavioural impacts, began to be observed and studied. During the 1990s, studies began to report that puberty was beginning considerably earlier than in previous decades, even as early as six or seven years of age in girls, based on breast development, although the age at menarche (first menstruation period) was later. Factors such as nutrition and social class have been cited as responsible for this change; however, there is still uncertainty about causes. Knowing about this is important because the early timing of puberty has been found to be related to negative psychological (e.g., depression) and behavioural (e.g., risky behaviours, acting out) outcomes, although considerable variability has also been noted in research. Impacts of puberty can relate directly to the brain changes that arise during that time and indirectly through the responses of parents and peers who observe the pubertal changes and behave differently towards the child (e.g., increase their expectations). Early puberty, technically known as premature adrenarche, is currently defined as occurring in girls aged eight years or younger and in boys aged nine years or younger. Puberty is no longer seen as a discrete or one-off event but rather as a process involving a series of changes in different parts of the body which follow their own pathway in a complicated way, with each aspect of pubertal development having its own unique meaning.

In her book titled *Tweens: What Kids Need Now, Before the Teenage Years* (2023), parenting educator Michelle Mitchell notes that tweens (defined as children between the ages of 9 and 12 years) are not the new teenagers, despite the real challenges they are experiencing in this specific stage of development. Importantly, she highlights that even when they come across teen-like issues, their stage of development means they are still thinking like children and trust in adults' ability to guide them. She describes this period as an opportunity for parents to "impress on their hearts who they are, the safe place they belong and an unwavering belief that their voice matters" (p. 213).

Understanding the human brain

The last two decades have seen new understandings about the human brain, particularly during early childhood, childhood and adolescence. It is now accepted that the human brain continues to develop well into our mid-20s (taking longer to fully develop in males than females), with changes occurring in peak periods such as puberty. We also accept that the areas of the brain that are most used are the areas that are likely to be strengthened, with pruning of underutilised areas. This is a very simplistic explanation of the complexities of the brain, and there is still much we are continuing to learn about the abilities and limitations of the child and adolescent brain, particularly as development and growth occur within the context of technology use. There is also a tension that comes with these discussions: if we don't expect much of our children because we believe their brain is still developing, we don't provide them with the opportunity to develop that comes from having expectations; on the other hand, if we are too critical of them or don't understand the limitations or weaknesses of the changes their brain is undergoing, particularly as they approach adolescence, we may be expecting too much of them, which is unfair to them and unhelpful to our relationship.

REFLECTIVE QUESTIONS

- What do you recall from your primary school years?
- Who did you talk to if you needed help or felt worried?
- How did you have fun as a child?
- Who or what were the biggest influences on you as a child?
- How is your child's life different from or similar to yours?
- How would your child describe their life?
- What are the signs of positive mental health you notice in your child?
- How are you actively helping your child to develop positive mental health?

CHAPTER 4

Making sense of technology use during childhood

While technology is now a key part of our lives and many aspects of our lives are enhanced by it, it does need careful management by us all. Unlike their parents and other adults, children have grown up with technology and don't know a world without the internet and mobile phones. This means that the way adults see technology won't be the same as the way children do, and this is an important starting point when thinking about how to understand and respond to technology use in children's lives. Being aware and confident as parents will help children learn to use technology well and come to their parents when concerned or uncertain. Unlike other aspects of life where experience counts, children will likely be ahead of adults in knowing about new technology. This creates risks, as parents may not be aware of how best to support their children.

A growing number of people in Australia and overseas argue that children shouldn't have access to smartphones and social media until they are 14 or even 16 years old (see "unplug childhood" - https://happyfamilies.com.au/unplugchildhood-org). Some of the concerns raised relate to research that links the deterioration of adolescent mental health to the advent of the smartphone. Other researchers question such a simplistic idea and point out that many other factors beyond technology alone have impacted on young people in that time. There's no doubt that technology has changed our lives, and I see impacts every day in my work that remind me of that. While I'm all in favour of children having a childhood that is rich in play and experiences in the real world, I'm afraid we may have missed the boat on banning technology. Even efforts to ban mobile phones in school become overridden when teenagers communicate with each other through their school-approved laptops under the eyes of their teachers. When banning anything, we tend to create a divide between those who ban and those who have been banned. Children and young people are savvy with technology and can find ways around the bans that adults aren't aware of. The last thing we need when dealing with such an important issue is a divide where opportunities to communicate and learn are lost. I believe that adults need to be very well prepared in understanding technology and be vigilant in monitoring children's use (which will include some restrictions). Having a balanced approach to managing technology is a more realistic approach, where both risks and benefits are understood and responded to in age-appropriate ways. The technology companies could help by building in mechanisms to promote children's safety, and this is an area in which governments could play a critical role.

Myriad uses and benefits of technology in our lives

Rapidly changing technologies mean that children are now able to use technology for multiple purposes - it can provide access to friends, entertainment and learning opportunities. They can access information and communicate with each other in ways that were not possible for their parents and grandparents. This can lead to new knowledge, access to information not previously available, and a future with new jobs in the information technology arena (using new technology that we can't even fathom yet). However, it can also enable children to accidentally or deliberately access information that may not be age appropriate. We are currently seeking to understand the impact of this on our children and our society.

I regularly read debates (on social media ironically) about the benefits and risks for children of engaging with technology from birth. Even preschoolers are now online, with varying degrees of supervision and interaction with parents. Every day parents and other adults are modelling to their children how technology should or can be used. Ideally, the modelling would also show when technology should be set aside or is not helpful. I see memes on Facebook of parents on their mobile phones and their children trying to get their attention. Unfortunately, I sometimes see that in real life too. I've seen a young child looking around a crowded medical waiting room to make eye contact with strangers, and the adults all totally consumed by their mobile phones and not noticing this bid for attention and connection. In that moment, I felt sorry not only for the child and the impact this might have on their growing awareness of the world around them and their place in it, but also for the adults who missed this opportunity to engage in a fun social interaction which perhaps represents the essence of our humanity, all for the sake of scrolling randomly into a distant world with questionable benefit.

How might technology use impact on children's lives and development?

Just what impact does all of this have on children's day-to-day lives, their ongoing development and the relationships they have with the most significant people in their lives, such as their family? It's early days and it's hard to know, but it's fair to say that while there are many positives, there are also some worrying signs we shouldn't ignore. Given the conflicting research, it's clear that we are yet to fully understand and integrate these new ways of communicating.

Increasing awareness about risks and concerns are leading governments and other authorities to consider bans on the use of mobile phones and social media by children and young people under 16 years old. Simplistic notions about banning are unlikely to be successful, yet it's clear that some forms of regulation are necessary to protect us all from accessing harmful content driven by algorithms that do not work in our best interests. A comprehensive approach that takes into account the pervasiveness of technology in the lives of children and young people, that includes regulation where possible, together with education and support, is necessary in my view to make a difference (just as we've seen with many other public health concerns – like addressing road safety by introducing legislation where appropriate, accompanied by improved safety mechanisms in cars, better roads, and effective public awareness campaigns that empower people through education and enable adults to model and support children in learning about how to be safe).

Risks associated with children's use of technology

There are certainly some risks that we need to be aware of and ready to ensure that children are protected from, including:

- **Access to content that may not be age-appropriate** (e.g., violent or sexual content). The risk attached to this will vary depending on the child's age, their interest in seeking out this content, and factors such as their personality. The younger the child, the more controls parents need to put in place to reduce the likelihood of access to violent or sexual content. Parents need to become informed about what might be seen online so they can provide guidance and support to help children make good decisions about how to manage their access to content.

- **Access to strangers.** This has been a longstanding concern for parents in the real world, and the online world leaves children vulnerable in what can be quite an invisible way. Ideally there will be controls and checks to ensure that children are aware of who they are talking to online and are only engaging with people they know. This is really the parents' responsibility to check, as children will be focused on playing the game (for example) and enjoying it and may not be aware of the dangers. Over time, talking with children to help them become more aware and able to take more responsibility will be critical, but even adults can experience difficulty in managing online contact with others. While it might seem that stranger contact online is less unsafe than in person, that's not the case, as considerable harm has been done when children have had contact with strangers who were perpetrators of child abuse in various forms.

- **Managing time.** Technology can take up a lot of time, which takes children (and ourselves) away from other activities, particularly physical activities and face-to-face social connections. While children may value spending time on technology, it is necessary that adults monitor this. It's up to adults to find a balance for their children between time spent on various activities. As they grow and develop, we can begin to share this monitoring role, but we have to be realistic about children's ability to manage their time on their own even into adolescence. Adults also need to recognise the strong drawcard that technology provides and ensure that children have opportunities to participate in other activities that are equally appealing to them.

- **Problematic internet use or possible addiction** – increasingly this is seen as a potential mental health disorder which needs specific treatment. There are signs that parents can watch out for that could suggest that internet use is becoming a problem – for example:
    - Spending time on the internet for longer and longer periods over successive weeks or months
    - Going online as soon as the child wakes up
    - Neglecting daily routines or responsibilities, such as homework or chores

- Minimising or lying about time spent online when asked by a family member
- Becoming irritable or aggressive when internet usage is curtailed or efforts are made by parents to time-limit software
- A drop in school grades, reduced ability to concentrate in class, or not completing homework tasks
- A noticeable decline in face-to-face activities, such as sports or hobbies or going out with friends.

When looking at these possible signs, remember that no two children are the same and their behaviour may vary, with some of these signs more apparent than others. In addition, some of these signs may not be related to technology use itself but be suggestive of other problems. If you notice several of these signs over a period of several weeks or months, it's worth considering the possibility that your child is experiencing difficulty managing their technology use and/or could be experiencing difficulties related to a mental health disorder. It can be difficult to tease out where the problem begins, and this is the challenge in research where it's difficult to identify the actual cause of the problem (e.g., children with mental health problems could be more likely to engage online as a way of coping, while being online a lot could cause mental health problems). Perhaps the reality is somewhere in the middle, as with many aspects of mental health.

Online social connections and relationships

While technology can provide opportunities to connect with friends and others with similar interests, as with other types of relationships problems can arise and children can experience harm. Cyberbullying and cyber-harassment are the areas of concern that we hear most about in relation to mental health and even suicide risk for children and adolescents in their use of technology. Cyberbullying and cyber-harassment involve the use of technology to cause harm to another person through comments, pictures, posts or sharing using emails, mobile phones, social networking sites, chat-rooms, websites and instant-messaging programs (basically wherever there can be online contact between people). Like face-to-face bullying, cyberbullying refers to repeated and deliberate behaviour where there is an abuse of power. It includes social exclusion, name-calling, lying or spreading rumours, threats to safety, impersonation, accessing accounts without consent, posting personal information without consent, and posting inappropriate or personal pictures without consent. This can be psychologically damaging and by its nature pervasive, following the child home and potentially impacting on them 24 hours a day.

Cyber-harassment can be a one-off, isolated experience, which can also be damaging to children and shouldn't be dismissed just because it isn't considered as serious as more ongoing negative interactions. Catching these experiences and acting early is important to prevent cyber-harassment from becoming bigger and even more impactful.

Gaming

Another aspect of digital technology that parents often worry about is gaming, and this continues to be confusing in terms of risks and benefits. In a recent book by Dr Alok Kanojia, titled *How to Raise a Healthy Gamer* (2024), the focus is helping parents understand what makes a healthy gamer and on restraint rather than restriction. As with other aspects of parenting covered in this book, the preferred approach is for parents to become informed first in order to understand and then to communicate and partner with the child to come up with positive solutions.

Parents are provided with a model of three components for responding to gaming:

1. **Education** – so that parents can understand why children are behaving the way they are.
2. **Talking to children** about the steps parents hope to take with them, including assessing their readiness for change and

building an alliance with them, using communication skills to connect with and ally with them (rather than going into battle with them).

3. **Action** – defining and setting healthy boundaries around gaming with the use of positive behavioural strategies.

The book includes an interesting section on the stages of change, which are often used in psychological approaches with adults who have longstanding patterns of behaviour, but not always considered when working with children. Given that technology use can become a pattern of behaviour that can develop quite quickly in children and be difficult to break, it does make sense to consider it in terms of how parenting approaches might work or not. Knowing which stage the child is in will also help parents to use different strategies. The stages could be useful to think about for your children:

1. **Pre-contemplation stage** – lack of awareness, frequent denial that a problem exists. Parents might try to convince the child that they have a problem and force change. A better approach is to use open-ended questions to encourage the child to think about the problem and remain non-judgemental about their technology use because they are not yet seeing any need to talk about it.

2. **Contemplation stage** – ambivalence or internal conflict starts to emerge. The child might be able to acknowledge that there are some advantages and some disadvantages, but the disadvantages aren't strong enough yet to attempt change. Parents in this stage might focus on the disadvantages and look for opportunities to create change when the child is still not fully in agreement. This can dismiss how the child is really feeling. It's better at this stage to sit with the ambivalence and continue to encourage exploration of both the advantages and disadvantages. Using reflective listening can here, as can voicing some of the mixed feelings, such as "You like gaming and it's fun, but sometimes it causes problems when you want to do other things too."

3. **Preparation stage** – the child acknowledges that it's time to change and that change can bring some positive benefits for them. At this stage parents can be so pleased that they jump to solutions or don't involve the child in planning for the change. A better approach is to work with the child to come up with some solutions and ways to change. Parents can offer choices and suggestions, but allowing the child choice will be more useful.

4. **Action stage** – everyone agrees it's time to make changes. It's important to note at this stage that even though motivation is high, it doesn't mean that there will be immediate or long-term success. Problems can arise if parents take over control and assume that the child will do what they say. It's better to agree on some boundaries and ways to manage the situation and encourage children to follow these while using open-ended questions to discuss any concerns that might arise. Checking in regularly and encouraging the child to talk about what's working and how they are benefiting from the changes can also be helpful.

Help and support for parents is readily available

The Office of the eSafety Commissioner (https://www.esafety.gov.au) conducts research and provides information and resources for children and parents. It's worth keeping up to date with the latest information available on their website and shared on social media. You will also see the Commissioner often in the media raising concerns and taking action to drive change with technology companies.

While this chapter has outlined potential harms and risks associated with technology use, it can be useful to remember that technology can also be used by parents to connect with their child. You can show genuine curiosity about how children are engaging with technology and always be ready to learn from them, whether this relates to a video game, an app they enjoy using, or a website where they are accessing interesting information. You can ask them how they are using technology at school and talk to the school if you have any concerns and require additional support. This will help your relationship by creating a common reference point, something to talk about and a way to be included in each other's worlds. By finding ways to enter into their world of technology, you are letting them know that you are aware of how important it is to them and opening the door more widely to their social world. They can also play the role of expert as they share information with you. This is important for their sense of self-worth and feelings of competence.

A useful resource for parents to help monitor and manage technology use by family members is the Family Media Plan developed by the American Academy of Paediatrics to assist families to use media thoughtfully and appropriately so that it can enhance daily life. This is an important tool to balance some of the simplistic messages about screen time that can be difficult to implement within the realities of daily family life. It also means you can monitor screen use over time, adjusting to changes in your children's stage of development and your family circumstances. Including children in developing the plan will also help them to see how important it is to actively plan for technology use and normalise this for the future. You can find the tool at: https://www.healthychildren.org/English/fmp/Pages/MediaPlan.aspx.

It can be useful to remember that while adults still seem to express ambivalence about technology, for children it is core to their existence. We are often focused on the negatives or what we think might be negatives, but in doing that we might be missing opportunities. By rethinking our attitudes to technology and keeping up with it, we might be able to find ways to use it to improve our lives and build closer relationships with each other.

REFLECTIVE QUESTIONS

- How do you see technology use generally? In your life? In the life of your family?
- What do you need to know more about in relation to children's use of technology?
- How do you feel about your child using technology?
- What bothers you most about the use of technology by your child?
- What approach to managing technology use have you used so far?
- How do you see the future of technology in your child's life?
- What role do you see for yourself in supporting your child?
- Is technology use by your child balanced between time with family, time playing outside, time playing with other children, and time alone?
- How much time does technology currently take up?
- In what ways is it helpful (e.g., for learning or playing with others) and how much is it isolating and stopping them from doing other things?
- What don't you know about your child's use of technology? How could you find out more?
- Who can support you with understanding and responding to technology use by children?

CHAPTER 5

Coping skills for a changing world

Living through a global pandemic provided us all with the opportunity to understand how closely our lives are connected with each other and with the natural environment. As we spent our days living a life that was disconnected from our usual places of support and entertainment, we had to draw on our inner reserves and find new ways to spend our time, to learn and have fun. Parents carried this load for themselves and their children. As we are now in a position to look back, we are seeing how parents of primary school-aged children were impacted by having to provide home learning while also managing their own lives, often working from home or facing the pressures of not having work. This time wasn't all bad though. Alongside these challenges, sometimes this extra time together was enjoyable and had benefits as daily life slowed and time took on a new meaning.

What has research told us about this time?

The Royal Children's Hospital National Child Health Poll in August 2020 titled "COVID-19 pandemic: Effects on the lives of Australian children and families" found that 42% of parents surveyed were more connected to their child, having spent more time reading (51%) and playing games together (68%) and 66% having developed new positive family habits since Covid-19. Families reported utilising digital media to stay connected with their friends and extended family (78%) and learn remotely (75%). Parents reported trying harder than usual to feed their children healthy food, with 63% of children being more involved in preparation of food at home.

As we now move away from the restrictions of Covid-19, we are no doubt still facing changes and uncertainties that weren't as obvious before the pandemic. Children's responses are variable. Some children are very aware of the past experiences, particularly if they missed school and their usual activities, and might even still be concerned about it happening again. With the passing of time, some of these concerns subside from consciousness or new challenges arise. Some children are sensitive to challenges facing their families, relating to financial pressures or family stress. Others are very aware of the world outside of their family such as the environment and impacts of climate change.

Impact of weather events and climate change on children

Children who have experienced the direct impact of natural disasters are obviously very aware of the ongoing risks associated with fires, floods and other weather events. Even children who haven't experienced these directly can be aware of the risks and may have worries about the future. In my work with children in Melbourne, I've recently seen children bothered by weather, such as heavy rain or wind. This can affect children's sleep and lead to a hypervigilance about weather changes. They can also become worried about noises or shadows. These worries can lead to them not enjoying their usual activities and even feeling embarrassed if they are aware that their reactions are different to other people's reactions to these events.

Parents can sometimes struggle to know how to support their children at times like this when they see weather as less of a threat. As with other difficulties children face, careful listening is a useful first step. Recognising that the fear and distress are real for the child, even when the actual risk is quite low, is an important first step to allow parents to listen and pay attention to what the child is experiencing. Working together to find out more about how weather works and to come up with strategies to help to manage the worries associated with the fear of impending events as well as during such events can be useful. This approach validates the child's experience while also helping them to learn to cope by feeling more empowered to deal with it with the support of parents. Taking it seriously and listening first is essential for this approach to work. However your children are impacted by weather events and other effects of climate change, becoming informed as parents about climate change can be helpful so that you are able to use accurate information when talking about it.

Coping with climate change and disasters

Knowing that children are aware and can become concerned or distressed can help parents be better prepared and open to noticing signs of concern early. In a book looking at children and climate change written by Ann Sanson and others (Sanson et al., 2022), the authors argue that coping with, or adapting psychologically to, climate change includes how children make sense of it, how they manage the associated feelings, and how they engage with the problem, responding practically, socially and politically. They note that research from Sweden in 2012 studied the way children from the average age of 11 to early adulthood were coping with emotions evoked by the challenges of climate change. They looked at three types of coping as ways that people cope with adversity and challenges:

- **Emotion-focused coping** – ways in which children try to regulate or eliminate uncomfortable feelings about the climate crisis. The researchers found that some children and young people used techniques like distraction, avoidance and deliberately thinking about other things. A smaller number (typically those showing low levels of climate concern) minimised or de-emphasised the severity of climate change, framing it as a problem that they don't have to worry about themselves or denying that it was happening. The most commonly used technique, particularly for younger children, was distancing from the worry. The researchers also noted that children used social support (talking to family and friends about their concerns) to regulate uncomfortable feelings. This style of coping was associated with higher levels of subjective wellbeing (compared to problem-focused coping discussed below) and also lower levels of environmental action, and served more to regulate worry than to promote hope for the future. In this way, while this type of coping helped the child feel better, it did not increase the child's involvement in doing something about the problem. Accordingly, it was a less constructive way of coping.

- **Problem-focused coping** – refers to children's efforts to solve the problem that is causing the stress. In the research children undertook both individual and collective pro-environmental actions and adopted these strategies almost as commonly as emotion-focused strategies to try to regulate worry (although younger children used distancing more than action). Individual behaviours included preparing for action (e.g., learning about the problem, planning what to do), and environmentally friendly actions (e.g., cycling to school, recycling, conserving household energy, and encouraging others to act). The collective problem-focused coping strategies included considering ways that problems can be solved more easily if people work together. Children who used this way of coping had higher environmental efficacy beliefs (i.e., believing they could do something about the problem). They were more likely to take action to protect the environment, but many of these children also expressed lower subjective wellbeing. This could be because when a problem is bigger than one person can solve alone, individual strategies can lead to feelings of futility and reduce wellbeing. Children who are actively taking individual action can express helplessness and exasperation if there isn't corresponding long-term action from the community.

- **Meaning-focused coping** – children use different ways of thinking about the problem of climate change to regulate their worry and promote hope. An example of this approach is positive reappraisal – reframing the situation to see its positive sides, like taking a historical perspective, noting how much more attention is now being paid to the problem than previously, or recognising that other seemingly insurmountable problems have been solved in the past through the sustained actions of committed people. Another meaning-focused technique was to deliberately cultivate positive thinking to promote hope. Children described trying to focus on the positive aspects and believing that the problem would be solved in the future. One child in the research said, "No hope, no reason to live." Cultivating trust in different societal actors such as scientists, environmental organisations, businesses, politicians and citizens working for climate solutions was another technique. This helped to build hope by recognising that millions of people worldwide share the same concerns and are developing new ways to address climate change. This helped children and young people to feel less alone with their concerns.

Children of all ages in the research reported using meaning-focused coping strategies, although less commonly than emotion-focused or problem-focused coping approaches. They used these strategies more to promote hope than to regulate worry. Younger children were more likely to use meaning-focused coping than older children, and their most commonly used technique was trust – and particularly trust in scientists.

The role of hope

Cultivating hope is another meaning-focused coping strategy. Three steps of active hope are:

1. Taking a clear view of reality
2. Seeing the direction the person would like things to move in
3. Taking concrete steps to change things.

How these work for children hasn't yet been researched. Researchers call it constructive hope when children and young people are able to face environmental risks and uncertainty, believe that their own actions and the actions of others can make a difference, and find positive meaning in action. By using their imagination, and then getting involved in action, children can cultivate hope. Encouraging children to imagine preferable futures for their community and then identify realistic steps to move towards them can stop children feeling helpless. Meaning-focused coping was related to several positive outcomes. Children and young people who used meaning-focused coping techniques also reported greater wellbeing and life satisfaction, a higher sense of purpose and optimism, and more active engagement in environmental issues, despite serious climate concerns.

Other research about coping is useful in understanding how children cope with a concern like climate change. Talking with trusted others and sharing and expressing difficult feelings have long been recognised as key to helping children to regulate their feelings. Research has found that a key factor was young people being able to share their feelings and thoughts without judgement with people who understand the issues. Engaging with nature is seen in research about how children cope with climate change, although it usually related to mental health and psychologically restorative benefits for children more broadly. This connection with nature has been called "wild hope" and described as a way of being and living that is rooted in nature-based experiences and contributes to a healthy present and future (Charles & Louv, 2020).

While these ideas about children taking action in relation to climate change (or other societal challenges) might seem unrealistic, it can be helpful to look at what actions children have been taking already. Collective action can build the belief that by working together on shared activities people can create change. This also helps children develop a sense of agency – the capacity and ability to take action by one's own free choices. A project by the Australian Institute for Disaster Resilience and World Vision Australia in 2020 involved an online survey on climate change, natural hazards, and disaster risk in Australia with approximately 1500 children and young people aged between 10 and 24 years. The survey data indicated that young people are deeply concerned about climate change, are concerned about how climate change will impact their own lives, and are more concerned about impacts that are far-reaching and universal. From their perspective, education has had a strong focus on causes and impacts of natural hazards but has not equipped them with the skills and knowledge needed to help mitigate the impact of disasters on themselves and their communities (Australian Institute for Disaster Resilience, 2020).

Including children in planning and activities can help them feel like they have a meaningful role to play during times of adversity and can offer psychological protection by helping them to feel more in control, more hopeful, and more resilient. No doubt the most well-known climate-change activity involving young people has been the School Climate Strikes, led by Greta Thurnberg, the Swedish student who began striking outside the Swedish parliament in August 2018 at the age of 15 years. Within a year, over 163 countries and up to an estimated six million people had participated in events (https://www.fridaysforfuture.org).

Supporting children to take action

Youth activism isn't without its challenges of course. In a study by Sanson and Bellemo in 2021, young people reported feeling immense pressure, feeling that all the responsibility to protect the future was being put on their shoulders, and risked burnout, mental strain and feeling overwhelmed. It would clearly be important for adults to work with children and young people to help them participate in realistic ways and maintain a balance between a focus on the here and now and the future. Just like adults, some children and young people will be more keen to become involved in action, whereas others may be less aware or open. If parents are informed and keeping up to date with local actions, they will be in a good position to talk with their children and tune into where their child is at in terms of interest and motivation. Looking at ways to be informed and take action as a family will enable children to feel supported at the level of engagement they desire. While it may be tempting to not talk with children about climate change, there is an argument put forward by environmental psychologists that trying to conceal the truth about the climate crisis can generate fear, harm a child's ability to trust, and skew children's objectivity about the climate crisis. This will particularly be the case as we all experience the impact of climate change in our daily lives, and children see weather events and disasters on the internet or news broadcasts. As with other issues, parents can tune in to their children's understanding and interests by providing opportunities for children to ask questions.

Role of parents in supporting children

Helping children find ways to cope with these uncertainties is important. We may think they're not aware of or affected by climate change, but they will likely be, in some way. It is best to begin with focusing on our own understandings, because our approach to understanding and dealing with these experiences will be reflected in the modelling we provide to children and the way we respond to them. Understanding ourselves first can help us become more aware of how we are feeling, how we are coping or reacting, and even to notice what might be obvious to our children. If we aren't taking the time to understand ourselves through our feelings and reactions, it will be difficult to explain to children what is happening and how we will manage, to be able to ensure that what we are showing our children is most useful, and even to have the ability to notice our children's reactions. In fact, noticing our children's reactions might give us insight into ourselves. They may be mirroring our reactions or reacting to us as much as to the actual situation itself that we are all dealing with. Knowing ourselves, particularly during times of challenge, and how we react to these situations, can help us understand ourselves more and in turn learn how to support children.

In order to fully understand and support children in relation to climate change, parents need to inform themselves and develop their own approach. Research has revealed how parents can be influenced by their children about issues such as climate change. In a study in the United States of 10–14-year-olds, parents' views were changed after their children were taught about climate change. Fathers and conservative parents showed the biggest change in attitudes, and daughters were more effective than sons in shifting their parents' views (Lawson et al., 2019).

Finding out more

A number of useful resources and groups are available to help parents:

- Parents for Climate: https://www.parentsforclimate.org/
- A guide for parents about the climate crisis – Australian Psychological Society: https://psychology.org.au/getmedia/f7d0974d-4424-4d60-a7eb-cfa0431b6860/parents-guide-climate-crisis.pdf
- How to talk to children about climate change – Australian Psychological Society: https://psychology.org.au/

getmedia/5f2f5be6-f710-46d0-9295-2004745561fe/24aps_how-to-ta 24aps_how-to-talk-to-children-about-climate-change-aps-toolkit-for-parents-and-caregivers.pdf

Children's worries about wars

The principles of responding to concerns related to climate change discussed above can also be applied to many other worries that children may have, such as worries about wars. As with climate change, children will respond differently depending on the extent to which they know about or feel affected by wars that are occurring in other countries. For children with family members living in areas where wars are active, their concerns may be specifically related to the safety and wellbeing of family members. For other children, seeing acts of violence through social media or news reports can be upsetting even if they don't have any direct connection. They may worry that what they see will happen closer to home. Just as with responses to weather events, the worry doesn't have to be actually real for children to become distressed and their lives affected.

Children may also hear other children or adults talking about wars and hatred at school and in the community. Depending on how parents have responded to these situations or the values that parents share about people from other countries or cultures, this can lead to confusion or attitudes that might cause conflict with others. Living in Australia provides us with the opportunity to connect and form friendships with people from a wide variety of cultural backgrounds. Knowing how to appreciate and respect this diversity is a critical skill that we all need to develop. In *Raising Antiracist Children: A Practical Parenting Guide*, Britt Hawthorne and Natasha Yglesias (2022) set out five principles for parents to keep in mind in understanding how antiracism can be enabled:

1. Community is at the heart of antiracism.
2. Children have a natural desire to learn.
3. Antiracism requires imagination, creativity and action.

4. An antiracist-prepared environment is imperative.
5. Re-parenting is required; enjoy the learning and unlearning that will happen.

It's clear from these principles that adults need to take the lead in order for children to develop awareness and behaviours that are antiracist and respectful of themselves and others, particularly those who are different to them. This begins with reflecting about the parents' and family's identity profiles to make sense of who they are in terms of their cultural background and other aspects of their identity. This includes individual qualities that make up a personal identity for each person, and a group identity that focuses on what the individual has in common with other people, such as age, gender, worldview, abilities and ethnicity.

Hawthorne and Yglesias also encourage thinking about social factors that relate to the way individuals can access support, and how laws and government or organisational policies might impact on them. This approach sits well with me as a community psychologist because it highlights how each of us exists as a unique individual as well as a member of a group and a society. Some people, because of factors outside of their own control, might experience life in that society as more challenging than others, and this can relate to experiences such as discrimination or racism. It's clear that discrimination and racism don't have to exist and can be prevented, but increasingly it seems difficult to understand what needs to happen to create a more harmonious world.

It's evident that it does need to begin with adults modelling respect for themselves and for diversity. According to Hawthorne and Yglesias (2022), parents should think about the messages they send their children about others. This includes approaches that encourage discussions with curiosity and honesty. A table in their book describes how awareness changes across childhood, with quite young children beginning to notice differences between themselves and other children, such as skin colour. They may show preferences for children who are like them because of familiarity rather than having negative thoughts about others. It's important to note that this early bias doesn't mean that babies are born racist. Rather, it can develop into racism if racial attitudes that adults hold start to be seen in the way that children see others, particularly the status of others. This highlights the importance of the types of conversations adults are having with children. Parents are key to this, but also the attitudes of educators and extended family members and the way they speak about and value diversity will be critical in ensuring that children learn about respect for others regardless of similarities and differences. Increasingly, it is recognised that open and explicit conversations about differences are necessary rather than more vague statements about everyone being friends. Helping children get to know other children from a range of cultural backgrounds and experience a range of cultural experiences can help them see themselves as part of a multicultural world and learn to respect others.

Helping children learn ways of coping with worries

Children being worried about climate change and wars overseas is a relatively new concern, but we know that children have always been worried about various aspects of their lives, particularly the things they least understand or don't think they have much control over. In her book *Coping in Good and Bad Times: Developing Fortitude*, Melbourne psychologist Erica Frydenberg (2022) tells us that coping is made up of our thoughts, feelings and actions in respect to the demands of our everyday lives. Coping becomes the way we deal with the world and the problems life dishes out. As we are all different and the situations we face are also different, she warns that there's no one formula for coping and no one right or wrong way to cope that will apply to every situation. Coping begins with an appraisal we make of the situation – the way we view the situation we are facing. We then choose to respond in a particular way. This is why people may deal differently with similar situations – because they think about them or interpret them differently. What one person sees as a major threat, another person may see as a minor irritation. Our past experiences, personality, and available supports can all play a role in how we firstly appraise the situation and then respond to it.

Erica's research over decades has explored how people cope. She found that people have many ways of coping, or strategies to use. She identified 74 different strategies, which could be further broken down into 19 strategy areas and finally into four coping styles:

1. **Productive coping** – working hard and solving problems while maintaining a social dimension or links with others as required. This includes physical recreation, humour, and seeking social support.
2. **Non-productive coping** – worrying, keeping to yourself, self-blame, wishful thinking, ignoring the problem and tension reduction. This can include drinking alcohol, gambling and sleeping, which can become a problem when used too much and interfere with healthy living.
3. **Optimism** – focusing on the positive, seeking relaxing diversions, seeking spiritual support and wishful thinking.
4. **Sharing** – sharing the problem with others, seeking professional help, taking social action, seeking social support, and not keeping the problem to yourself.

Optimism and sharing are generally productive and helpful, although it's always useful to remember that an excess of anything can lead to problems. For example, only sharing problems and never trying strategies can lead to a sense of helplessness or dependency on others and not contribute to learning from experiences to improve the capacity to cope in the future. Different strategies may be helpful for some situations and not others, so it's useful to reflect on what has proven most useful and to consider what it was about that situation at that time that made the strategy work. We can help children to begin to reflect on these ways of coping, by modelling as well as actively teaching and encouraging children to try out strategies for themselves. This can then set the scene for discussions and feed into problem-solving and conflict resolution. Being confident in having the ability to cope with problems can build a sense of competence and contribute to hopefulness.

Opening up a conversation about worries

When we are trying to help children cope, it can be useful to have a list of gentle questions to help open up the conversation – use open-ended questions rather than questions that children can say yes or no to. You might also suggest that they draw a picture or show you by using their toys. It can also help them to draw or play as you talk:

- When you said ... just now, can you tell me how you're feeling? I'm wondering if you mean ...?
- I've noticed that you look a bit sad lately – would it be OK if we talked about it? Have you been feeling a bit sad?
- If you are worried about something, who are the people you could tell?
- You seem a bit grumpy lately. Sometimes people get grumpy when they're worried about something. What are the biggest things that you are worried about today?
- Everyone has worries sometimes. What would your biggest worries be today?
- When you just said that you wanted to die, I got worried and would like to help you. It's important that you are safe and I'm here to help you with that. Can you tell me what you were feeling when you said that? What happened that made you feel like that? Have you had those feelings before?

This approach might feel uncomfortable if you haven't been talking with your child about feelings before this (or are uncomfortable with your own feelings). A useful book that can help is *How to Talk So Kids Will Listen and Listen So Kids Will Talk* by Adele Faber and Elaine Mazlish (2012). The first chapter of the book, titled "Helping children deal with their feelings", will be a useful starting point. The authors describe a simple process to help children with feelings:

- Listen with full attention – put away other distractions and focus.
- Acknowledge the feelings with a word – be specific.
- Give their feelings a name – come up with the name together so it makes sense to them.
- Give them their wishes in fantasy – this helps to acknowledge what the child wants to happen.

The authors also remind us that sometimes presence and comfort are desired, without words. This can help a child feel supported and less alone with their worries. This warm and responsive approach, known as co-regulation, can help children learn better ways to regulate their emotions during times of upset. Co-regulation is described by Lauren Marchette, a psychologist and lecturer in psychiatry at Harvard Medical School, as "connecting with a child who's in distress and being able to evaluate what that child needs in the moment to help calm themselves … The tricky part of co-regulation is that adults have to recognise how they're feeling and be able to regulate their own emotions in difficult moments so they can help children to gain these same skills" (Salamon, 2024). Sit with your child and be guided by their interest in talking, using gentle prompting rather than trying to force the conversation. It can take time for you both to get used to talking and listening in ways that are different to how you might normally communicate. It's worth persevering and setting the scene for future conversations by letting the child know you will be there with them. This is important for them now and will set the scene for an open and trusting relationship in adolescence.

REFLECTIVE QUESTIONS

- What explanations do you provide your children about climate change and events such as wars?
- On a scale of 1–10 (1 being not ready at all, 10 being very ready), how well prepared are you feeling about talking with your children about these events?
- What approach are you likely to take in helping children learn to cope?
- What experiences do you have of being helped to cope with a difficult situation?
- How did adults support you to cope during your childhood?
- What were your typical coping strategies as a child or teenager?
- What are your main coping strategies now as an adult?
- Is your approach to coping different as a parent to other situations in your adult life?
- Do you have one main coping style to deal with situations?
- How do you see your role in helping children to cope?
- What do you notice about your child when you try different strategies?
- What approach seems to work best with your child to cope with situations?
- What do you notice about your child's ability to cope? Do they sometimes surprise you with the way they deal with situations that arise?
- When does your child seem to cope best?
- What simple day-to-day experiences can you begin to practise with?

CHAPTER 6

Getting along with others

One of the joys of childhood can be feeling part of a group and playing with friends. On the surface this can look easy to do, but for many children it can be quite difficult to make and keep friends. It actually requires quite a lot of social and emotional skills to be able to know what to do in the first place to make friends and then how to manage the many difficult scenarios that can arise. For adults as well as children, being with others requires us to place our own needs on hold in order to be present and considerate of another person, or people if in a group. This is where our social and emotional skills can be really tested, because it requires us to be both aware of our own needs and feelings as well as to manage them while thinking about the other person. Some children seem to do this easily, while others struggle. We often notice this struggle when the child is upset or argumentative. It's harder to notice when the child is withdrawing or always giving in to others. Parents can observe these times by watching their children during play and also by asking how they are enjoying playing with their friends. You can ask curious questions about what games they play, who chooses the games, what happens if there is a disagreement, and how the child is feeling about playing with other children. Even asking if they like being in class or recess or lunchtime best can elicit some of this information. You might also notice the child's behaviour when they are talking about other children or when a play date is planned. Through this process, you might see some patterns emerging – for example, the child enjoys structured games better where the rules are clear, the child copes better playing 1:1 rather than in a group, or the child gravitates to younger or older children.

Social development skills

Getting along with others requires children to have a range of skills that can be taught. Helping children decide who to play with may also be helpful. Some children will rush in to play and not be too fussy about who they play with. Other children can be quite particular about wanting to play with a certain child. This changes over time, with younger children playing alongside others and then over time making more choices about who they want to play with. As children develop in their own ways and according to their own timeline, sometimes there can be a clash in how this works in a group of children. Understanding where your child is at in relation to their social development can be helpful. Here's a rough guide to help you.

Social development skills by age

Approximate age	Social development skills
5–6 years	• Follows simple rules and directions • Learns adult social skills like giving prizes and apologising for unintentional mistakes • Likes to spend more time in peer groups and being part of a group of friends • Imaginative play becomes more complex – likes to dress up and act out fantasies or concerns

Approximate age	Social development skills
7–8 years	- Understands rules
- Shows a deeper understanding of responsibilities related to relationships
- Begins to complete simple chores
- Moral development continues
- Learns more complex coping skills
- Explores new ideas and activities; beliefs and values may be tested by peers
- Identifies more with other children of the same gender and may find a best friend
9–12 years	- Peer and group friends begin to take precedence over family
- Shows increasing independent decision-making and a growing need for independence from the family
- Develops an interest in community activities and adult relationships outside of the family
Adolescence	- Develops greater independence and commitment to peer groups
- May indulge in risky behaviour to explore uncertain emotions and impress peer groups
- Social interactions include complex relationships, disagreements, breakups, new friends, and longer-lasting relationships

You can see the gradual development across the childhood years of the way that relationships are seen and developed. It is important to note that there is a wide range of differences among children in their development of the skills required to manage the complex nature of relationships. Children are exposed to many different social situations and relationships within their family and extended family, and with their neighbours, other children, and adults in education settings. Learning about others adds to their knowledge about themselves and helps them to see themselves as part of a family and community. Parents play a critical role in modelling and facilitating these different relationships, providing a scaffold to help children understand what is involved and then slowly allowing more independence. It may also mean at times advocating with others about what the child needs.

While humans are hard-wired to be social, children, just like adults, will respond differently to social situations through their personalities and temperaments. Children with autism spectrum disorder will need more support in social settings. This includes helping the child as well as others to learn how to most effectively get along. Children who enjoy sport might be particularly interested in being with others so they can enjoy playing the game. Children who are more introvert in their personality may be less open to large groups or constant companionship. Children who have experienced bullying may be reluctant to trust again or may be defensive when meeting other children, in order to protect themselves from other bullying occurrences. Our job as adults supporting children is to take all of these possible aspects into account to help them understand themselves and how relationships work. Observing the child and taking note of how they are responding will help parents to better understand their child and help them feel comfortable and confident in the various social situations they find themselves in. Seeing social development as a crucial part of a child's development is important for parents, and this might also mean reflecting on how friendships and relationships work in parents' own lives, given the important role that modelling plays.

Friendships during childhood

Another way to view social development is through a closer look at friendships with other children. Based on the work of Robert Selman, a five-step framework is helpful to see the progression over the child's development.

Behaviours by stage and approximate age

Stage and approximate ages	Behaviours
Level 0 friendship: Momentary playmates – "I want it my way" (3–7 years)	• Children view friends as momentary playmates, and their friendships are all about having fun together. • Friends are children who are conveniently nearby and who do the same things they like to do. • Children have very limited ability to see other perspectives. They assume that other children think the same way they do and can get very upset when they find out that a playmate has a different opinion. • Children may say "She doesn't want to be my friend anymore" when their friend wants to do something different to them.
Level 1 friendship: One-way assistance – "What's in in for me?" (4–9 years)	• Children understand that friendship goes beyond whatever their current activity is, but they still think in very pragmatic terms. • They define friends as children who do nice things for them – such as sharing a treat, saving them a seat on the bus or giving them nice presents – but they don't really think about what they themselves contribute to the friendship. • Children at this level care a lot about friendship. They may even put up with a not-so-nice friend just so they can have a friend. • They also may try to use friendship as a bargaining tool, saying things like "I'll be your friend if you do this" or "I won't be your friend if you do that."

Stage and approximate ages	Behaviours
Level 2 friendship: Two-way, fair weather co-operation – "By the rules" (6–12 years)	• These children are able to consider a friend's perspective in addition to their own, but not at the same time. • They can understand turn-taking, but have difficulty stepping back and getting an outsider perspective that would help them to see patterns in interactions. • Children are very concerned about fairness and reciprocity, although they can think about these concepts in a very rigid way, and can be very judgemental of both themselves and others. • They often invent "secret clubs" involving elaborate rules and lots of discussion about who is or isn't a member, although these tend to be short-lived.
Level 3 friendship: Intimate, mutually shared relationships – "Caring and sharing" (8–15 years)	• Friends help each other solve problems and confide thoughts and feelings that they don't share with anyone else. • They know how to compromise and do kind things for each other without "keeping score" because they genuinely care about each other's happiness. • This can also be a "joined at the hip" stage. Girls, more often than boys, may be best friends and expect each other to do everything together. • They feel deeply betrayed if a best friend chooses to be with another child.

Stage and approximate ages	Behaviours
Level 4 friendship: Mature friendship – "Friends through thick and thin" (12 years and up)	• Children place a high value on emotional closeness with friends. They can accept and even appreciate differences between themselves and their friends. • They're also not as possessive, so less likely to be feel threatened if their friends have other relationships. • Mature friendship emphasises trust and support and remaining close over time, despite separations.

SOURCE: KENNEDY-MOORE (2012)

Your child's personality is necessarily going to impact on their ability to make and keep friendships. Children who are more sensitive can be caring about their friends and acutely aware if a friend says or does something that is hurtful. A child who is less sensitive may not notice or may let this go. Impulsive children tend to act before thinking and this can impact on those around them if they are not aware of other people's needs. Children who have siblings or socialise a lot with other children are more likely to understand sharing than a child who has less exposure to other children on a day-to-day basis. An ability to share is a necessary component of making and maintaining friendships.

Adults' role in helping children develop friendships

It can help children to learn to play with other children when adults facilitate the process. For example, a parent might encourage a child to notice other children, and to speak to them. Parents are constantly modelling this kind of behaviour, so taking notice of your own responses when in public settings, at the school or with family is a good starting point. Attitudes towards others can also come into play, so it can be helpful to notice your attitudes to others, particularly people you may not know or might not get along with. If you are openly critical in front of your children about others, your child may learn to judge and criticise others. On the other hand, if you are friendly and respectful, giving people the benefit of the doubt, your child will pick up on these values.

Helping children to learn that other children might not see things the way that they do is an important part of being able to make and keep friendships. This ability to see that others think differently is called "theory of mind" and it's an important ability that can sometimes need active teaching. If we assume that others are thinking the same way that we do, we will become easily frustrated if they don't do what we think they should do or if they want to do something differently. Whereas, if we recognise that they may not understand the world in the way we do, we might be able to take a more curious stance and wonder what they are thinking. We might even be open to recognising that their ideas could be good and worthy of consideration. Teaching our children this ability is essential for them to function in a social world. Guiding children to think about other people's perspectives and using stories to explore different responses and thoughts of characters are ways that children can become more aware that others might see the world differently.

Understandings of gender and sexuality

Navigating relationships can also include age-appropriate understandings of gender and sexuality. While it may be tempting for parents to delay talking with their children about sex until they get older, there's increasingly a recognition that these conversations need to start early and continue often. There are a few reasons for this – children have always been naturally curious about their bodies and sex, children are exposed to information about gender and sexuality that can be difficult for them to understand, and children who are aware will be in a better position to protect themselves and seek help if they are uncomfortable with others' behaviours. You may have your own memories about this curiosity and how you sought out information. The way this curiosity and need for information is handled can lead to children thinking about sex in different ways. If their curiosity is responded to well and they are provided with useful information that helps them feel good about their bodies and how they relate to others, it can be helpful. This sets a solid foundation to build on where parents can continue to add more detailed and specific information over time. If, on the other hand, children are faced with opposition or a shutting down of information, they can learn that this is a topic that is off limits, not to be talked about at home. This won't stem their interest, and in fact it might make them even more curious and interested in finding out more while not able to approach parents to find out what they need to know.

Sexuality education

When I was growing up, parents talked to their kids about the "birds and bees", a once-common euphemism for sex education. In those days, the focus was often on biology and keeping safe from pregnancy and sexually transmitted diseases. During the last two or three decades, the focus has shifted to also including information about human relationships and the importance of respect in these relationships. While this began to provide a more comprehensive approach to sexuality and human relationships, it still seems way too simplistic compared to what children need to know about today. We are now much more sophisticated in our understandings of sexuality and gender, with a greater appreciation of diversity. We are well aware that not all people will be heterosexual and that people can be homosexual or bisexual. We also know that some children are transgender and there is a growing understanding and acceptance of this in schools and communities. Despite this increased awareness and growing acceptance, pressures on children who are gender diverse continue to be extreme and adequate research is yet to be undertaken, partly because it is quite hard to get accurate data. Although there's little focus on children and gender diversity at present, adolescents with gender diversity are now known to be at a higher risk of mental health problems and suicide, and it's reasonable to think that children who are gender diverse or gender questioning could also be at higher risk, even though data collection and research is yet to catch up with this.

Talking openly and honestly with children about sexuality and their understandings and encouraging their questions will help children know that you are prepared to have these conversations. This can be challenging and many parents feel uncomfortable about this topic. Recognising that part of children's development, even from a young age, relates to sexuality will help to remind us that this is important, and as much as we might like to we can't ignore it. Ensuring they have access to credible and up-to-date information will be important, particularly if you feel uncomfortable. Being mindful of the way you speak about homosexuality will be important, as children who are aware of their sexual diversity will be looking for signs of how acceptable this will be to share with their parents. Jokes or comments which suggest that you are not approving or can't understand sexuality other than heterosexuality, for example, will serve to silence children who are uncertain about their sexuality. This can leave them feeling unloved and disconnected.

Children also need to be prepared for issues like sexting (sharing of sexually explicit images through technology), which can, like cyberbullying, cause distress. Talking with children about the importance of respecting others as well as themselves will be critical as core values, which can then be translated into online relationships and activities such as sexting. It's also important to know that sexting is likely to increase among children as technology use increases and may be seen as normal by them rather than problematic. Talking to children about how it may become a problem in the future, for example, can help to ensure they are aware of potential risks that they may not have thought about. As with other behaviours, it's important to be non-judgemental if children share their experiences with you. Instead, work with them to understand what happened and work out how to do things differently if necessary in the future.

Perhaps the main difference now to decades ago is that children can access information online. Before the internet, the most we might have found when trying to learn about sex would be dictionary definitions or perhaps a *Playboy* magazine. Now there's a wide range of information that can be accessed, with children left to make their own sense of it. In her recent book *Talking Sex: A Conversation Guide for Parents*, Vanessa Hamilton (2023) reminds us that children are getting a sexuality education every day from the world around them. She asks parents to think about whether that is the type of education they want their children to receive. She also sends a very clear message that providing this education is the parents' responsibility to ensure that children have the best opportunity to be safe and healthy.

It can be difficult for parents to know where to start when thinking about sexuality education and they can often feel unprepared and uncomfortable, perhaps not having received very useful sexuality education themselves. As with other topics in this book, parents can begin with reflecting on their knowledge and experiences and then become informed in order to be better prepared to support their children. Thinking about sexuality education as more than just conversations about sexual intercourse will be helpful. Sexuality education relates to understanding gender and gender roles, views and feelings about oneself and one's body, as well as sexual relationships with others. This can be seen as a gradual process for children to learn and experience, beginning with initial awareness during the preschool years and expanding over time to be more complex. This complexity relates to our understandings as well as the tendency for concepts that were once clear now being less so. If we take gender, for instance, it's clear now that gender is not as simple as the sex that a person was born with. Even young children sometimes question their gender, and there are debates worldwide about how parents and medical professionals should be responding to children who express a need and desire to be a different gender.

Sexuality education for children has the following aims, according to Hamilton (2023):

1. **Learn** – cognitive, emotional, physical and social aspects of sexuality
2. **Aim** – equip with knowledge, skills, attitudes and values that will empower them
3. **Consider** – how their choices affect their own and others' wellbeing; understand and protect their rights
4. **Realise** – their health, wellbeing and dignity; respectful social and sexual relationships.

Looking at sexuality education this way reminds us of just how core it is to the lives of us all and how necessary it is for parents to support children from an early age to begin to learn and importantly to open the door for communication over time as the child's needs and interests continue to develop.

Although it may feel instinctual to protect children from what we consider to be unnecessary information, it's important to know that children are at risk of accessing information that relates to sex from other children or the internet. If they don't have some basic understandings, they can become confused and even ashamed, which sets the scene for difficulties in the future. However, if they have some context and feel comfortable to raise this with parents, they can be supported to make sense of it.

Maree Crabbe is an Australian researcher at Queensland University of Technology whose research has focused on the use of pornography. She found that among young people who had seen pornography, the average age of first exposure was 13.2 years for males and 14.1 years for females. She highlights that while that is the average age, some children are exposed much earlier – for example, children with other siblings may unintentionally be exposed to pornography. Curious children may also deliberately seek out information and access pornography online, or they might accidentally click on an internet pop-up or web search. They might also be shown it by someone else or see it on social media. In an article in *The Conversation*, Crabbe and her fellow authors (Flood et al., 2024) argue that pornography shapes young people's sexual understandings, expectations and experiences, just as it shapes these among adults. Like Hamilton, they argue that children having access to sexuality education is a critical strategy to mitigate against pornography exposure, along with parents being equipped with the tools to talk to their children about pornography.

It's important to also recognise that some curiosity and contact between children of a sexual nature is very normal and doesn't always need to be a concern. To help parents understand when to be concerned and how to respond, Hamilton (2023) uses an ages-and-stages approach to outline some of the typical behaviours of children. If parents are aware that this is normal and part of children's development, they will be able to respond in a way that is positive and does not shame or embarrass the child. Talking openly about privacy and respect for each other's bodies will be helpful as an opportunity to start conversations that are comfortable and encourage children to be able to talk freely when they are curious or concerned. We protect children best when we have open conversations from a young age. This obviously means parents needing to be comfortable with these kinds of discussions, in a way that may not have happened during their own childhood.

Body awareness and body image

We might think about body image issues as a concern among adolescents rather than children; however, research in Australia and internationally has recognised body image concerns among children as young as eight or nine years. Research from the Murdoch Children's Research Institute and the University of Melbourne (2018) found that girls tended to be more dissatisfied with their bodies than boys, but boys with higher hormone levels also felt unhappy with their physical shape. The researchers used a tool called the Kids' Eating Disorder Scale to measure body dissatisfaction.

This comprised eight illustrated silhouettes of children ranging from very thin to very obese, with separate sets for females and males. The child was first asked to select the silhouette that most looked like them now (self-rating) and then asked to select the silhouette they would most like to look like (ideal rating). Each silhouette was scored, and by subtracting the ideal rating from the self-rating children were allocated either a positive or a negative body satisfaction score. Hormones associated with puberty were measured through saliva. The study's findings suggested that the vulnerability to poor body image and dissatisfaction appeared to be linked to hormone levels associated with the onset of puberty. They found that the higher the level of hormones, the more unhappy the children were with their body size. As children with heightened levels of hormones also tended to be taller and heavier than their peers, it was suggested that this could be the cause of their poor body image, as they felt more conspicuous about their bodies in comparison to their peers.

Body image is another one of those topics that we are yet to fully understand, although considerable research is underway. It involves the way in which children see themselves (related to self-worth and identity) as well as actions that arise from a desire to improve the way they look. It highlights what can happen when the body and mind connect. There's no doubt that the media play a role in this in the way that males and females are portrayed, particularly when images are photoshopped to show unrealistic and impossible body shapes and sizes. This affects both males and females, and it's not surprising that these images begin to influence ideas about what is valued in our society when children are seeing them from a young age.

We know that among adolescents and adults body image concerns might not just be about physical appearance. They also might have something to do with self-control and self-loathing. Psychologists have theorised that people may control their body as a way of feeling better by gaining a sense of control when a lot of things are spiralling out of control. It's incredibly complex, and as with other issues it will also need to be explored with the individual directly to fully grasp what it means at that time for that person. While we don't yet have research that supports that this is the case with children, children with body image challenges need professional assessment to understand what's going on and provide support. As with other issues, the earlier this occurs the better the chances of effectively making a difference. When this impacts on eating, there is a risk that an eating disorder (such as anorexia nervosa, bulimia, or binge eating disorders) might arise. The risk of other mental health problems and an increased suicide risk is high for people with eating disorders, and increasingly funding is being allocated for research and treatment of these conditions.

Given this complexity, what can parents do to prevent their children from experiencing body image issues or eating disorders or to respond to them when this occurs? Here are some suggestions:

- Talking about balance and moderation and having a lifestyle where this is modelled is helpful as a starting point. One of the challenges with this, however, is that a person with body image issues, and particularly with an eating disorder, may have a different perception of what is balanced. Arguments about balance and moderation within that context are likely to cause frustration and even risk worsening the situation.
- Use media images and messages as a springboard for discussing healthy body images with children. Discuss media messages that are inaccurate and unhealthy as well as positive media images.
- Help children understand that their bodies will change and grow, particularly at times such as puberty.
- Help children understand that there is not one ideal body shape.
- Watch out for comments that children make about their own and other people's bodies.
- Avoid stereotypes or using words such as ugly and fat.
- Help children focus on their abilities and personalities rather than their physical appearance.

- Discourage children from weighing themselves too often.
- Exercise may seem like a good thing to do, but excessive exercise may become problematic. Much of this may be hidden for some time, and this adds to the challenge of tackling it effectively. Careful monitoring of exercise and encouraging a range of activities, including some "down time", may help.
- Seeking professional advice about any concerning signs you are seeing may be necessary.

It's interesting to note that we began talking about social developments and the importance of making friends and ended up talking about some aspects of friendships and relationships that can be challenging. Friendships take skills to develop and maintain and may involve managing difficult situations. Helping children to learn about this and being prepared to support them when concerns do arise will help parents feel confident and continue to prioritise the role that social development has in children's lives, now and in preparation for the future. Having friends and social support can help us during times of challenge and can help us to remain hopeful and positive about our lives.

REFLECTIVE QUESTIONS

- How would you describe friendship?
- What do you recall about your own friendships during primary school?
- What helped you to make friends?
- Was it difficult or easy for you to make and keep friends?
- How would you describe friendships in your life at the moment?
- What are your expectations about your child's friendships?
- What messages do you send your child about being a friend?
- How do you approach difficulties your child may have with friendships?
- How have you provided information and support to your children about sexuality education?
- What concerns you about talking with children about relationships and sexuality education?
- What is your approach to helping children learn about their bodies?
- In what ways do you model healthy attitudes to bodies and sexuality?

CHAPTER 7

Appreciating attitude – encouraging children to speak up and find their voices

It's not too long ago that children were expected to be seen and not heard. While we might not see this as part of our parenting style now, there continue to be remnants that flow through in the way we see the place of children in our lives. It can be easy for adults to dismiss children's ideas or to think that adults always know better. In my experience with children and adults, I don't think this is always the case. Sometimes children can see what adults can't, or don't want to, see. While they obviously don't have the life experience of adults, they often see with a simplicity and clarity that we lose as we move into the complex world of adulthood. Children often tell us what they think in a direct and honest way without the complications that adults sometimes add to our communication. It's one of the reasons I continue to enjoy working with children in my psychologist role - their comments or feedback can be pretty brutal at times, but

I certainly know where I stand, what they are thinking, and what they like or don't like. That helps us to move forward together faster than when there's too much over-thinking, worrying about what the other person will think, or thoughts about what should be said or done.

I think there's also an irony when we think about children having a voice and speaking up. We often encourage children to speak up to others, stand up for themselves, and let others know what they think. We might not like it so much when they speak up to us, though. We might describe it as "talking back". It's at those times when we might find ourselves returning to the old-fashioned "children not being heard idea". We might be keen for them to speak up to others or in situations when we think they need to speak up, but not to us. Of course there's more to it than this, and it helps children to learn when to speak up and when to listen or go along with others. There's a place, however, for us to help children learn to be assertive and to have the confidence to share their ideas. It is helpful to remember also that being assertive means thinking about yourself as well as the other person.

Speaking up is one way that children can feel empowered and feel heard and valued – in the places we want them to speak up in. Often in my work with adults we work on assertiveness skills: what it means to be able to say what you are thinking in a way that is clear and also respects the other person. Many people never learned to do this growing up, and some may not feel sufficiently worthy to do it as an adult. To be assertive we need to feel that we have a place, that we are valued and that others respect us. Otherwise it's easier and can feel safer to be submissive and keep quiet. Sometimes it's just not possible to do that, and we can become aggressive and angrily let people know what we think. Perhaps the least helpful approach is when these ways of communicating blend together and passive aggression is the outcome – when underlying feelings and thoughts are silenced yet body language or behaviours demonstrate that the person has some strong feelings. This might lead to "silent treatment" or subtle acts of aggression. It's difficult to have open and authentic relationships when people feel like they can't speak up and say what they think.

Benefits for children of speaking up

There are many benefits of speaking up for children, particularly in a world that is changing and uncertain. If they can speak up, they can feel like they are more part of the world around them. It can reduce their worries and anxieties, because they can voice what they are thinking and talk through ways to deal with various situations. Adults are not always aware of just how alert children can be about situations around them. They can be worrying about things that parents didn't even know they knew about. Sometimes they overhear something that concerns them or hear part of a conversation and start to make sense of it for themselves. Sometimes they can pick up on feelings or what is not said. Like adults, they can be tuned into body language and recognise when people are not happy or feeling worried. I see this in my work with children when I ask a child and their parents to complete separate self-report checklists about aspects of their mental health. It's very common for children to score higher on some of these scores than parents, because it's just not possible for parents (or anyone else) to know everything that is happening for another person. While this can be confronting at times, it can also be a significant breakthrough for parents to start to understand that their child may be having some experiences that they haven't known about. To fully understand and support their child, they need to be able to encourage the child to speak up and be ready to listen and hear what is happening for the child.

Home is the practice ground for children to learn the skills of speaking up. This means at times they'll go too far, saying something hurtful or not listening enough to others. This can give parents the opportunity to help children learn, through listening and validating and sharing what it's like for others when they say those things or use that tone. Communication between humans is complex and requires nuance to pick the timing, the words, the body language and the tone that is appropriate for each situation. Some of this is unconscious, so our job as adults supporting children can be to help them become more aware of how their communication is helping or not helping. Valuing what they have to say, while encouraging them to value what others are saying, underpins this.

Encouraging children to speak up

If you want to encourage children to speak up, there are ways that you can support them to learn this skill:

- Recognising the courage it takes to speak up and take the risk that others might not agree or might be unhappy with us
- Choosing the best words to express ourselves to another person or group of people – adults do this all the time through modelling, so becoming more aware of your own communication patterns and habits can be a good starting point
- Knowing what is important enough to speak up about – helping children to clarify ideas as they make sense of the world around them
- Picking the right time to speak up – for example, setting up times like dinner time when time is made for everyone to share what they are thinking
- Being prepared for a range of different responses and being able to make a decision quickly to deal with them – this can include learning that others might disagree or not feel the same way about a situation
- Finding a way to speak up while also thinking about the other person's feelings and needs.

You might be thinking that these are skills that take a lifetime to develop, and even then it is hard to always do it well. No doubt you've had experiences when you didn't speak up and wish you had, or when you chose to speak up and wish you hadn't. Learning how to navigate this begins in childhood and continues to develop over our lifetime. Parents are modelling all the time when to speak up, how to do it, and what to do if it goes badly. You might be aware of your tendency to do this or not. If you find it difficult, you might want your child to be able to do it, but not be sure about how to help them. If you do it and think it's important, you might already be encouraging them to do likewise. If it comes easily to you, you might forget how hard it can be for others.

Your child might be keen to speak up or might be hesitating. If they are hesitating when you find it easy to do, you might find it frustrating and wonder why it's so hard for them. This is where the child's personality can come into play. Some children are more outgoing, while other children are quieter. Some children jump into situations without too much thought, whereas other children take a while to warm up and need more time to plan and build up their confidence. Finding some middle ground here is probably helpful – taking some time to think about the situation but not so much that the moment is lost or it becomes stressful. Practising at home is helpful, and there are day-to-day ways you can help children to speak, such as asking them questions that encourage them to think about their experiences (e.g., instead of "How was school today?" you could ask "What was the best thing about school today?", "What was the most interesting thing you learned at school today?" or even "What didn't you like so much about school today?"). This may seem like a small change, but it can encourage the child to think a bit more deeply to come up with a response, it shows interest in their day in a more genuine way, and it allows the child to develop their critical thinking skills.

Providing opportunities at home for your child to find their voice is an important starting point. If they can't speak up at home, they are unlikely to feel like they can speak up in other settings. If children speak up and are shut down by their parents or their ideas are joked about or criticised, they will learn very quickly that they don't have anything worth saying or they shouldn't be speaking because people don't value what they say. This can then be interpreted as not being valued as a person, leading to low self-worth. This feeling from childhood can continue into adolescence and adulthood, with the risk that the person as an adult continues to feel devalued and unable to speak up, in some cases even to meet their most basic needs.

The idea of "mattering"

Mattering, according to Prilleltensky and Prilleltensky (2021), consists of feeling valued and adding value. Feeling valued means being appreciated, respected and recognised. Adding value means making a contribution and making a difference in the world. People feel valued by, and add value to, their self, relationships, work and community. Prilleltensky and Prilleltensky argue that mattering is essential for happiness, health, autonomy, self-acceptance, wellbeing, purpose, mastery and growth. They also claim that beyond personal outcomes mattering is also crucial for justice and community wellbeing, and when feeling valued and adding value are balanced, a healthier society can be built.

When I first read about these ideas of mattering I felt like I knew it already somehow, that it was something I had taken for granted or known that it's there although not always visible. Perhaps it's something we notice when it's missing – we might notice it when we feel like we don't matter to others, that what we do and say doesn't matter or make a difference. The authors warn us that mattering faces a serious challenge in the future as robots and artificial intelligence eliminate millions of jobs and people find it difficult to make money and meaning. I wonder, though, if mattering faces an earlier challenge than that for children if they don't feel like they are seen and heard. Perhaps it's always been a challenge for children.

Mattering could be a useful way for us to reflect on how we help children have a voice, feel like part of the family, school and community. It might help us to understand behaviours, as

Prilleltensky and Prilleltensky state that a great deal of human behaviour can be explained by the need to either feel valued or add value. They argue that some behaviours are driven by the pursuit of a positive experience, like feeling valued or adding valued, while others are driven by the avoidance of a negative experience, like feeling devalued. They go on to say that everyday interactions at home, school, work and in the community involve mattering, with a wide range of interactions. Some might be very brief but can be memorable and impactful.

If we think about children's behaviours, we might be able to see how they want to be noticed by adults and how their efforts to be seen might work or not. They might be trying to help or contribute, or they might be more focused on themselves. Their efforts might be appreciated by those around them or dismissed. This might then affect how they see themselves and how they behave in the future. This sense of mattering or not can affect the way they see the world around them and their role in it. Feeling hopeful about the future no doubt requires us to feel like we have a place and some significance to others.

The self-fulfilling prophecy

Children are absorbing all the messages they receive from others, particularly parents, so it makes sense that they will be heavily influenced. Of course the self-fulfilling prophecy works in both negative and positive ways. If children receive positive messages about their capacity and their abilities, they will feel more confident in themselves and have a go at new things, which in turn can build their confidence and competence. If they receive negative messages, including being shut down when they speak up, they will take on the message that they are not worthy or can't do things.

A classic study from the 1960s by Rosenthal and Jacobsen provided evidence for this self-fulfilling prophecy, which they called "the Pygmalion effect" (1966). They conducted their experiment at a public elementary school, where they chose a group of children at random and told teachers that these students had taken the Harvard Test of Inflected Acquisition and been identified as "growth spurters". They explained that these children had great potential and would likely experience a great deal of intellectual growth within the next year. They gathered performance data on all the students and compared the students described as "ordinary" with the "growth-spurters", finding that the students the teachers had expected to do well (the "growth spurters") actually did show greater improvement than their peers. The children hadn't been told of their false test, so the researchers concluded that the teachers' expectations had influenced student performance. Based on this research, it follows that adults' expectations of children can make a difference to children's ability to do things and to believe in themselves.

Using "teenage attitude" to communicate

Children are beginning to show what adults consider to be "teenage attitude" from increasingly younger ages. As they become exposed to media and social media, they are learning different ways to communicate and even to challenge their parents. Parents can respond in different ways to this newfound attitude. Ways that encourage the voice and embrace it within caring limits are likely to do better, with fewer arguments and more benefits for the child as they learn how to communicate their ideas in ways that others can hear. Parents who try to shut their child down are likely to have more conflict and also not help their child to learn how best to communicate their ideas. This begins with an attitude from parents that it's good for children to speak up and that when they do so they aren't being disrespectful. Harnessing the child's voice and helping the child to use it well could be seen as the job of parents. A useful approach could include:

1. Acknowledging that you have heard what the child said
2. Asking the child to talk more about it
3. Exploring together where the ideas came from

4. Suggesting that you might have some ideas to share as well
5. Offering some ideas about how they might improve the way they spoke (if necessary)
6. Together coming up with a plan about what to do next (if anything)
7. Thanking them for sharing.

Helping children to feel confident to speak up is critical to their development. While in previous decades adults were assumed to know what was best for children, it is clear now that this is not always the case. When it comes to safety, adults may need to have more of a say but even then it can become easy for adults to over-protect children rather than encouraging them to work out how they can keep themselves safe in different situations. Young children from early childhood are now encouraged to say what they need and what they think to adults. This is seen as core to their healthy development and learning about themselves as individuals as well as being part of a family or group.

Speaking up as a type of risk-taking

Speaking up involves risk-taking to some extent and it's possible that over recent decades parents have generally encouraged less risk-taking by their children. If your child is having difficulty speaking up because they don't like to do new things or take risks, it can be useful to encourage activities that stretch their abilities and encourage them to try new things with scaffolding. In her book *50 Risks to Take with Your Kids: A Guide to Building Resilience and Independence in the First 10 Years* (2021), Daisy Turnbull encourages parents to explore challenges with children to build physical skills, social confidence and character development. She recognises the need for parents to think differently about their children and move outside of their comfort zone in order to do this. This includes allowing children to find their own solutions to problems and parents enabling children to find their confidence in being able to do this.

It's important to think about risk-taking as sometimes doing things that we might not consider to be much of a risk. One of the concerns that children often bring to me in my work as a psychologist is a worry about speaking in front of their class. I'm often reminded of my own experience as the new girl arriving at a new school and standing in front of the class to be introduced to the other children. I remember feeling very self-conscious and have a vivid recollection of becoming aware that my foot was moving out of my control. I still recall that feeling of being looked at and potentially judged, that feeling of wishing the ground would open up below me and empty me into it. Over the years, I've learned to manage that kind of anxiety, and public speaking and presenting is now one of my favourite work-related tasks. When thinking back to that little new girl, I wish she had known what I now know – others aren't noticing everything I think they are and they also feel the same way. Helping children learn this takes time and practice. Some teachers are very good at recognising how difficult this task can be for some children and are able to find ways to scaffold the task of presenting, allowing children to begin to share in a small group, read out from their seat, stand with the teacher, and then over time work towards the experience of standing in front of a class and talking. For some children this can become a form of social anxiety, as they worry so much about what others will think of them. They may have had an unfortunate experience where they felt genuinely embarrassed or were laughed at, so their fears may be real. Helping children learn to speak up in a range of environments, practising at home, and helping them learn that others won't care as much as they think and are probably nervous too, takes time and patience from adults. Underneath all of this, the idea that they have value and they matter to important people in their lives will give them a sense of confidence that will help them learn to take the necessary steps to perform in front of others.

REFLECTIVE QUESTIONS

- What questions or ideas did you have as a child?
- How were you able to speak up as a child?
- Who listened to you when you attempted to speak up?
- How do your childhood experiences help you understand your ability to speak up now?
- What are your thoughts about children speaking up?
- What efforts do you make to encourage your children to speak up?
- What do you notice about their ability to speak up at home and in other places, such as at school or with friends?
- What else can you do to encourage your child's confidence to speak up?
- What concerns you about your child's ability to speak up?
- Do you see risks in encouraging your child to speak up?
- How can you ensure that a child's ideas are heard and valued?

CHAPTER 8

Supporting children through hard times

Every family will face some hard times, and children who are well supported during those times will be able to manage the situation and even learn (and ideally grow) from the experience. Past generations have tended to protect children from difficult or sad situations and not include them in plans or discussions. While well-intentioned, to help children maintain their childhood innocence or not be burdened by the challenges of life, this could have had the opposite effect and left children unsupported and feeling left out. Often children are aware when something is wrong. They often pick up on parts of conversations or notice their parents' changing behaviour. They might then try to make sense of the situation themselves, which might lead them to think that something totally different (or even worse) is happening. Ironically, efforts to protect children by not sharing any information can lead to them feeling more worried or upset (and isolated) than if they were included and provided with age-appropriate information while also being enabled to get on with their day-to-day life. Our approach now is to better understand the needs of children and to include children as much as possible, taking into account their age and stage of development, their personality, and their preferences. We understand that resilience comes from an ability to cope with difficulties with the support of others as well as drawing on our own resources.

Helping children understand death

Beginning with day-to-day conversations can be helpful to set the scene for children to understand and be prepared for situations that might arise in the future. If we think about death, for example, we can make use of stories to explore what it means to die. Children are naturally curious, and it can help to use their questions as guides to know how much information they need to understand something. The younger they are, the fewer details they might need, but sometimes even quite young children want to know exactly how things work. Psychiatrist Irvin Yalom, in exploring children's understandings of death from an existential perspective, describes parents' attempts to manage their own anxiety when confronted by children's awareness about death:

> *Generally parents attempt to assuage a child's fears by offering some form of denial, either some idiosyncratic denial system or a socially sanctioned immortality myth. What an investigator discovers, then, is not a child's natural inclination but a complex amalgam consisting of a child's awareness, anxiety, and denial intermingled with an adult's anxiety and denial defences (1980, p. 82).*

If we shy away from issues like death we are potentially setting up a situation where children learn that these are not topics that our family can talk about. Then, when faced with the death of a pet or grandparent, there's no strong foundation to draw on. It's much easier to talk about a topic like death when we aren't in the midst of our own sadness and grief. Having a book or story can help to ground you and the child and use something familiar to build a sense of comfort and safety for the child. It can help to have language to use that we don't need to find for ourselves, particularly if we are finding the topic challenging.

Supporting children through sadness and grief related to death forces adults to confront their own ideas, and even fears, about death. As children ask us questions about what happens when someone dies, where they go, and what it will feel like, we are confronted with the need to find an answer when we might rather not talk about it. Perhaps in fact we've found ways to avoid thinking or talking about it until their persistent curiosity means we can no longer ignore it. Children have a way of confronting us like this – at these times they leave us with a simple choice: we can embrace the question and use it as a chance to learn more about ourselves, supporting the child in the process, or we can shut down the conversation and continue to avoid it, teaching them in turn to avoid hard topics.

Thinking and talking about death can be hard. If we have strong religious or spiritual beliefs, it might be much easier because we'll have a model to draw on, with concepts and language that will help. If, however, we don't have such strong beliefs or we are questioning beliefs that we were taught as children, we might struggle to understand death ourselves, let alone explain it to a child in a way that makes sense. We may have experienced the death of pets or people in our lives, and how that was handled at the time will affect how we now feel about death. For example, if your grandparent died and your parents showed their distress, talked about the grandparent, and encouraged discussions about memories of the grandparent, you will have learned that death is something that can be talked about – perhaps even as a way to honour and respect the person beyond their death. If, on the other hand, your parents and family members experienced their own grief in a way that was problematic for them, any discussions may have been silenced, and as a result you may not have had the opportunity to ask those curious questions. You may even still have questions about what actually happened.

Most parents I work with now are keen to encourage discussions about death. Unlike in my childhood, when at the age of 12 years

I was excluded from my grandmother's funeral, typically, we are now more open about children attending, and being involved in, funerals. Perhaps we have learned that the approaches of previous generations to shut down hard discussions can leave us floundering decades later. Excluding children from events such as funerals can be dismissive of the child's grief and need for support. Funerals and other rituals are ways of being together with others who cared about the person who died, and can form a significant component of the grieving process. By excluding children, it's as if children have no feelings and somehow don't need the support that adults are receiving. Not all children might want to go to the funeral, but that doesn't mean they don't need support or some other way of marking the death. Understanding how to talk with children and monitoring their responses will help to know what will be most helpful for each child.

Planning to talk with children about death

If you are finding it hard to think about having these discussions with your child, here are some tips to help you make a plan:

- Prepare as much as possible before you are faced with death – you can begin with day-to-day experiences, such as how plants live and die. Talking about plants dying and not being able to be revived can help children understand the permanence of death. Younger children may find it hard to understand that death is permanent, so having tangible examples can be helpful. You can expect different responses from different children, with some showing quite a lot of emotion while others might be more dismissive. It's important not to push any particular feeling, just to share your thoughts and feelings and encourage the child to take notice and be curious. You can then observe how their interest or responses change over time.
- Discussing the cycle of life can be useful, and even young children can grasp the idea of changes happening over time. Talking about a person being born, then living a life, and then

eventually dying can help children make sense of the world around them. It can also help them to value and appreciate life and the importance of living each day as well as we can. Noting that while most people live into older age, sometimes people die earlier, can be important. Children will often ask parents about when they will die and may be anxious about their parents dying. It is best not to make any promises but rather to say that hopefully we will live for a very long time and have lots of fun together. This can be reassuring while also acknowledging realities and uncertainties associated with life and death.

- Be clear with language when talking with children about death. Avoid using euphemisms like "passed away" or "in a better place". This leaves children wondering what you mean and even misunderstanding what you are trying to tell them. It can be more frightening and confusing when messages are unclear than receiving the news more directly. Children often cope better with clear facts than adults do.

- When breaking news about a death to a child, choose a quiet, familiar place if you can. You might think about ways to help them feel safe, such as having a favourite toy nearby. Plan what you will say and allow time for the information to sink in and for the child to ask questions. Be ready to share that you are feeling sad. Explain clearly that when someone dies, their body stops working, they can't eat, walk or play any more, and the child won't be able to see them again. Beyond that, be guided about the amount of detail the child needs by listening to their questions and watching their reactions. Be prepared that they might appear uninterested after a short time but could ask questions later. This is very normal and the way that children process information. Their reactions may change over time and they may ask questions when you least expect them. Showing a willingness to answer the questions as best you are able to will be important, rather than focusing on what the correct answer should be. It's OK to say that you don't know something. Some things you might be able to work out together, but some questions might not have clear-cut answers. It's important to allow the child to feel safe and comfortable to ask any question and have the time with you to talk it through.

- Use picture books to create opportunities to explore ideas about death and how people understand and cope. This can help to give you a reference point for questions later and remind children that this is a topic that can be discussed.

- Bear in mind that children may sometimes think that things are their fault. For example, a child might have thought something mean about a person who then died and might therefore believe that they caused the death. Being clear that there was nothing anyone did that caused the person to die will be very important in a situation like this. Noticing a child's reactions and asking them if they have any questions or worries will help the child to feel comfortable to share this worry if they are thinking about it.

- During the early days following a death, try to stick to routine as much as possible. While there may be some disruptions, try to prioritise what the child needs in terms of meals and bedtime and favourite rituals to help them feel safe and secure. These routines will also be helpful to you.

- It is normal for a child to show some behavioural changes during times of change or stress. This can include regressing to old habits, like thumb sucking or "baby talk", or "acting silly". It is best to notice and monitor this rather than trying to change it. You can reflect how the child might be feeling as a way to acknowledge them, name the feelings and help manage those feelings. Routines and comfort will be most helpful. As things settle again, the regressed behaviours are likely to disappear. If they continue, it can be useful to talk to school staff about any changes that may have occurred at school as well. You could also increase time together and encourage the child to talk, draw or play in a way that helps them express their feelings.

- Be open with your own feelings. Let your child see you crying and talk with them about how you are feeling and what is helping you. This is modelling for them about how emotions work and what we can do with them. You can normalise the way that crying works to release our feelings and can help us to feel a bit better afterwards.

- Consider whether the child should attend a funeral, taking into account the child's age, temperament, relationship with the person who died, and interest in attending, as well as who else will be attending. Prepare your child for what will happen at the funeral so they can feel prepared and included. You could ask your child if they would like to draw or write something about the person that can be shared. If they do attend, make sure you have a plan for who will be with the child and can help them leave to take a break if necessary. You can always plan your own small memorial for the person if the child doesn't attend the funeral. There are many options, and remaining focused on the child's needs and interests will help you make the best decision at the time.

Separation and divorce

With almost 50,000 divorces taking place in Australia in 2022 (and 127,161 marriages), it's clear that separation and divorce are fairly common and likely to involve children (Australian Bureau of Statistics, 2022). Obviously there's more to this than just these point-in-time numbers – not all parents are in a relationship or married, for example. We also don't yet know the impact of Covid-19 on relationships and whether this trend is going to change in the future. For some families, the pandemic – particularly lockdowns – placed family members under incredible stress. Other families may have managed better or relationships may have strengthened, as was found in some of the research referred to previously.

In any event, relationship problems and conflicts in families create a lot of stress and uncertainty for children. Hearing parents argue or fight, being caught up in arguments or not being able to do things because of the conflicts – all impact children significantly.

This experience can make a child's life difficult during childhood, and the effects can continue into the way they see themselves and how they understand relationships in the future. It can be very difficult for children's needs to be met when parents are having problems in their own relationship. Children may feel alone with their worries or ignored. Behavioural problems may start to occur, such as becoming withdrawn, and the child might then become the focus and potentially even be blamed for the family's problems.

Given that stress in families is common and conflict can occur when separation or divorce is occurring, what should parents do to protect their children from further distress?

1. **Keep the needs of the children at the centre.** This can help to refocus the parents' attention back to the children, which they both have responsibility for. This focus can help with priorities and provide opportunities to maintain the sense of identity as parents with an important role in the lives of their children.

2. **Seek help for the adults' relationship and learn communication skills that are respectful and effective.** This not only reduces the conflict at home but also models to children how to communicate well in a relationship. It is often the way that communication occurs that escalates tensions and conflict. Children can easily pick up on these tensions, even when parents think that they are not hearing or aware. Even young children can respond to the body language of adults.

3. **Share only what is necessary with children about the adults' relationship.** Providing children with too much information about the arguments can be overwhelming and lead to children feeling like they need to take sides between their parents. There is also the risk of "parentification", where children take on more responsibility for adult issues than is appropriate. Sometimes children in that situation feel pressure to fix the problems between the parents. When this is impossible, they can feel self-blame or responsibility for the relationship breakdown.

4. **Observe children's reactions when the family is together.** If you notice the child's behaviour changing (e.g., getting louder or quieter, talking less to one parent, making comments about the family's functioning), take this as a cue to act. Talk with the other parent and then follow up with the child about how they are feeling, and work on recognising patterns of communication that have been unhelpful and making changes to ensure that children feel safe and comfortable when the adults are together. Sometimes this requires support from others to enable children to be protected from adults' conflict and tensions (e.g., staying with extended family members or friends).

5. **Be guided by children's questions.** Create an environment in which any question is a good and important question, and use this to help you understand what your child is needing. Remember that this will change over time as children develop. They may seem to be asking the same questions again and again, and while this might seem unnecessary to adults it is a sign that children don't have the answers they need yet or are at a different stage in their cognitive development so are starting to see things differently or needing additional information. It could also mean that the explanations provided to date haven't been sufficient or tailored appropriately to meet their needs and help them feel secure. It's important that children's questions are never silenced but are embraced as a sign of the child's curiosity and need.

Impacts of family violence on children

Ideally children live in families where respect and safety are prioritised. Unfortunately, however, sometimes children are exposed to family violence, including physical, sexual, psychological and financial abuse. Ensuring that a child is safe from this abuse is a priority and always an area of focus for me in my work as a psychologist. In fact, I – and teachers and others who work with children – am ethically and legally required to report to child protection authorities any situation where children are not being protected from harm. Supporting children to have a voice and ensuring this is heard is a priority at times when there is conflict or aggression in the home. Letting them know that their safety is important is critical. This can be more difficult than it sounds, though, as children will have loyalty to each parent and will be trying to find their own ways to keep their relationship alive with each parent. Sometimes they will show ambivalence and worry about what to share with the other parent.

We know that children's mental health and development is severely impacted by witnessing and experiencing family violence. This can lead to behavioural issues as children act out what they are experiencing, having learned that aggression is the way to deal with conflict or to get what you want. They might withdraw and shut down at places outside of the home because they have lost their voice at home and don't feel like they have any worth. They can begin to show signs of trauma, including nightmares, hypervigilance and problems with attention. Many of these trauma responses can continue into adulthood, and we now know that many mental health problems in adults are related to experiences of childhood abuse and neglect. The Australian Child Maltreatment Study found that child maltreatment is very common in Australia, with 62.2% of participants reporting that they had experienced at least one form of abuse or neglect before they were 18 years old. The study also found that those who were maltreated were significantly more likely to have a mental health disorder in adulthood and to experience health risk behaviours, including self-harm and suicide (https://www.acms.au).

This is an incredibly challenging area and complex for parents to navigate because it involves caring for themselves and their child, as well as negotiating their way in the relationship. Seeking professional support is very important to ensure that both the adult's and the child's needs can be prioritised. Recognising the signs early and reducing the impact can mean that longer-term effects of experiencing family violence will be minimised. Support can be obtained through a number of helplines and services available nationally:

- 1800 Respect: 24/7 phone line and website: https://1800RESPECT.org.au
- Relationships Australia: https://www.relationships.org.au

There are also a range of services in each state and territory that can be helpful. The above services will be able to provide details, or you can do an online search for family violence services in your state or territory.

As children become exposed to issues facing the world such as climate change and wars overseas, as well as violence much closer to (or at) home, they can become concerned and distressed. If children are exposed to family conflict or experience bullying, we need to be aware of the significant impact this can have on them and actively prevent these experiences from occurring or continuing. Ensuring safety (both physical and emotional) is critical for children's mental health. If the adults around a child dismiss experiences where children aren't safe or don't provide opportunities to check in and hear what they are thinking or worried about, children have to find ways to manage this themselves. This might show up in acting-out behaviours or through withdrawing and internalising their feelings. Then adults get stuck in having to develop responses to fix the problem. We know now that children benefit from adults who listen and help them, providing structure and guidance that is tailored to the individual child and is adapted as they develop. The days of children being seen and not heard are long gone, yet the after-effects of this approach can still be seen.

REFLECTIVE QUESTIONS

- When you have experienced hard times, what has helped you most?
- When you think about hard times and children, what is your first response?
- What is most difficult for you when you think about supporting children during hard times?
- What helps you to care for yourself during hard times?
- What experiences do you have that you can draw on to support yourself and your children during hard times?
- What messages do you receive from others about how to support children during hard times?
- What worries you most about your children during hard times?

CHAPTER 9

Recognising and acting on early signs of mental health concerns

While we can do much to support children's positive mental health, there will be times when it's clear that children need additional support. Mental health concerns in children will show up in their behaviour and ability to cope. Signs may also come through in play or things they say to you or others. Perhaps you have noticed some changes in your child's behaviour or their ability to cope with the daily challenges they face. Maybe getting to sleep or staying asleep is difficult. They may be eating more or less than usual, or eating could be becoming a source of conflict. Their tolerance for others may be lowered, and you may notice they react differently to how they did previously. Some of these changes could be quite normal, and even a healthy part of the child's development, as they are learning to assert themselves or respond to situations. However, these could be signs that there is a need for some support in understanding what might be going on and in reducing any longer-term impact.

Understanding mental health concerns in children

As is the case for everyone, there is not just one factor that leads to mental health concerns. Sometimes these are related to their earlier experiences, such as changes or traumatic life events. Sometimes they are related to the child's temperament and sensitivities. Some children pick up on things that other children don't even notice or worry about. They may face challenges at school with learning or with friendships. It's easy for adults to minimise the difficulties children face. It's also easy for us to draw on our own experience of childhood, or perhaps draw on idyllic ideas about childhood being a carefree time. It can be distressing for parents and other adults to see their child struggling with worries. Understanding the child's development and looking at ways to listen and hear about the child's experience will be helpful. The earlier we notice and respond to children's distress, the more easily we can create changes.

As we've seen already, mental health difficulties don't just arise from nowhere, although they may seem to at the time. Often there has been a period of struggle that may or may not have been visible to adults, and during that time communication and trust might have been breaking down. As children develop, becoming more independent and responsible for themselves, communication will change and it can sometimes be difficult for parents to know what is happening for their children, and particularly to distinguish between what is normal and what is becoming a concern.

When children are younger, they often seek adults out when they are feeling sad or upset. We may be in tune with them to the point that we also can pick up on signs about how they are feeling even if they don't tell us. As they grow, our job as parents is to help them develop the skills to take more care of themselves. We expect them to tell us how they feel if they need to, but we also expect them to take more care of themselves, working out their own solutions and being able to deal with their feelings in better ways than when they were younger. What can be missed in this scenario is the extent to which children still need us, even though they may appear more independent and capable. Add in a busy family life and pressures from school and friends, and we begin to set the scene for a perfect storm with struggles and breakdowns in communication. This is no doubt exacerbated by children's increased use of technology, which can create new problems and may remove them from regular conversations with parents. Now, it's important to recognise the various circumstances that have led to this point without blaming ourselves and becoming overwhelmed with guilt – though this is much easier said than done.

Finding ways to connect to deepen understandings

Start by setting the scene to have conversations and finding ways to do this that fit in with your family's lifestyle. Finding genuine ways to connect will be important so the efforts don't seem token. This will take time and may not work as quickly or easily as you'd like, particularly when your child is feeling down and stressed. Breaking patterns of communication that have developed over a long period takes effort and time. Some questions to consider when planning how to do this:

- Look for connecting points – what do you and your child both like to do or talk about? What interests do you share (or have shared in the past)?
- What are the simplest, cheapest ways you can connect with each other?
- How can you create space and time for each person in the family to have 1:1 time with parents as well as time as a family group?
- When are the best times to connect – over breakfast or last thing at night? Does this vary across the week?
- What have you noticed about your child's efforts to connect with you? When does this happen? What do they do? If they haven't done it recently, what have they done in the past?
- Given that technology is such an important part of life, how can it be used to help you connect?

- How can food make connection easier?
- What settings help the conversation flow more easily? (For example, does going for a drive or a walk work better than sitting facing each other?)
- Are there television shows or movies that you can watch together that you can both enjoy and talk about later?
- What might you need to give up for the moment in order to build these times and spaces for connection? What has got in the way of your connection?
- If your child was asked how they would like to connect with you, what would they say? Can you ask them? If not, why not? What concerns do you have?

Building trust as a way to enable communication that feels safe

When we are able to communicate more effectively, we will be in a position to rebuild trust. Trust can break down when we feel like we have let each other down. We may feel like our child has let us down through their actions and not telling us how they've been feeling. Our child, equally, may have felt let down if they attempted to tell us or sought help from us and felt unheard. This is good to know, but we should try not to feel guilty about it. Guilt will close down the relationship and not enable trust to develop or be regained. It can help to think about how trust develops in a family situation. It's one of the essential elements of a family that's working well, but it's very common for it to be tested as children develop. Parents may struggle with trusting their kids when they break rules, for example. From a child's point of view, it can be difficult to feel that parents don't trust them, and sometimes this can lead to resistance and rebellion. It can be easy for a vicious cycle of trust developing and breaking to occur. Finding ways to regain trust and work towards trusting again are important aspects of parenting.

A few conditions are essential for trust to be developed and maintained:

- **Unconditional love** – this seems like a natural way for parents to love their children but can be difficult in reality. Children may feel like our love is conditional on them behaving well or doing things that the family can be proud of. Exploring what this means together can be critical for moving forward during difficult times, particularly if there have been arguments and critical or hurtful things said in the heat of the moment. It's a paradox of parenting that because of our love for our kids we can sometimes come across to them as judging or blaming them or not caring about them.
- **Honesty** – this is the basis of positive relationships, of course, but going through phases of lying and keeping some things secret are part of a child's healthy development as they test out new ways to do things or observe our reactions. Children who are worried about getting into trouble are more likely to use lying to protect themselves.
- **Reliability** – this can be as simple as following through on what we say we will do. Again, this may sound simple but can break down quickly if circumstances change. Creating ways to communicate effectively if things change can help here – for example, explaining what happened and acknowledging the child's feelings.
- **Empathy** – concern for the needs of others. This requires the ability to think about what is going on for the other person and what they might need from you.

Recognising when things escalate

Sometimes even young children can think about dying or hurting themselves. In the event that a child is talking about wanting to die or hurt themselves, it will be important to act more quickly, beginning with asking the child what they mean and what is happening to make them feel that way. Listening to understand what is happening for them is critical here, as is seeking further support. Although it's not openly discussed at the moment, children can become suicidal and even die from suicide. It is confronting for parents to hear their child talking about wanting to die, and one of the ways that parents try to deal with this is to try to shut down the conversation or tell the child they don't mean it or they are being silly. These responses don't help the child to explore why they feel so distressed or to see the parents as a support. That in turn can leave them feeling more distressed. Jumping ahead of the following steps by reaching out to the school, making an appointment with their general practitioner, and taking them to see a psychologist would be useful if the child is talking about wanting to die. Calling the Kids Helpline (https://kidshelpline.com.au/) together could also be a useful first step.

The value of seeking help early

We absolutely know that seeking help as early as possible is very important. For children, this can mean early in age as well as early in terms of signs of concern. It's particularly important because mental health concerns can impact on the development of children. It's easy, however, to get caught up in the confusion about what might be a "stage" or "phase" of development and what might actually be a sign of an emerging mental health issue. This is challenging to tease out, because many of the behaviours are the same, and when you combine that with the child's personality and life circumstances there's a bit to untangle. As a parent, we are part of that tangle, bringing our own personality, reflections and life experiences too. That's why it's so useful to receive help from a mental health professional. By seeing the situation from a neutral and distant place and bringing to bear their training and previous experiences of working with other families, mental health professionals can bring a whole new perspective to increase our understandings. They can ask questions to get us thinking about those things we tend to ignore or may not be aware of. These questions and observations can help to lift the lid on what is happening for us. As long as we are open to the experience, this can provide new insights that can help us to understand what is going on more easily. Sometimes this is difficult because we tend to shut out what is hard for us to face.

Seeking help when you notice signs of concern

Even after professional help has been obtained, parents, along with other family members and friends, play a crucial role in supporting their child. While parents might feel helpless and believe that they aren't able to provide the help their child needs, in fact the opposite may be true. The child will benefit from having family members who are supportive and physically and emotionally present with them. You are the constant in their lives and know them better than anyone else. Even when the child is seeing a mental health professional, family members will be the people the child has day-to-day contact with. You are the people who will provide most of the support. This can at times feel overwhelming, particularly when you feel uncertain about what to do. Having some agreed plans about what to look out for and how to respond if the child becomes distressed can be helpful.

It can be helpful to bear in mind that this is something you will have been working on with your child since they were young, so it won't be new. You might be tempted to think that they should know how to manage strong feelings and solve problems by now or even that some ways of resolving problems are obvious. Remember that this may not be as easy as it looks, and when distressed it's common for funnel thinking to kick in, which reduces the capacity to think of all options. Making decisions when emotions are heightened is difficult for us all. Helping children to think through the steps of making decisions and working through problems can be something that you model and work with them on a day-to-day basis. Being patient with them and showing that there is always a range of options for any problem can be helpful. One of those options is that they can always ask others for help if they need more ideas.

Getting started in seeking help

There are some general rules that we can apply to make a decision about when to seek help. Generally speaking, it's much better to reach out for help earlier rather than later, particularly for children, whose development can be impacted considerably when they are struggling with managing their daily life. If the changes or concerns have been present for a couple of weeks without an obvious cause, exploring this further would be a good idea. Sometimes there is a reason, such as a change in the family or school routine (a parent or teacher being away, for example) or the child having been unwell. In those situations children can be sensitive to what is different, and behaviour or mood changes can occur. These will typically settle when the child adjusts or when the situation settles. Sometimes these changes might be less obvious, and could be related to something like a parent being worried about something and being less focused, which the child can pick up on. So the first step is to consider what's been happening lately, to try to identify when the concern first began and what was happening at that time. That in itself might prove useful, and you can then talk with the child and work together on ways to resolve the situation.

If there's no such obvious change or reason, it would be useful to check with the school to see if any changes have been noticed there. This might provide the teacher and other staff with the opportunity to consider if anything has happened at school that could be impacting on the child and also to share any observations they have made. Often working together with the teacher can be helpful. Establishing a way to communicate regularly (e.g., regular email contact or a communication book) can be a helpful way for you and the teacher to share if you have noticed anything unusual and also to notice and build on what is working. Sometimes a meeting might be needed to allow time to explore the issues and come up with a plan for how the school and family can work together. Developing this relationship with the teacher during difficult times will be easier if parents have already been engaged with the school in a more proactive way. Parent engagement is described by Stewart (2023) as giving "your attention to the learning process and to the growth and progress of your child, making an effort to support them, through your active participation and interest as they move through school" (p. 139). Being engaged and seeing ourselves as active participants in children's learning can help to build trust with educators, which can prevent difficulties arising and also provide a safe pathway to accessing support when concerned.

Understanding the mental health system

If the reasons for the concerns have been explored and efforts to support the child have not been successful, the next step would be to make an appointment with your general practitioner. Ask for a longer appointment to talk about mental health so that you aren't rushed. Make a list of your concerns and what you have tried. Be prepared to talk about any family factors that could be relevant, including a family history of mental illness. The general practitioner will want to rule out any physical health concerns first so may take some blood tests. If there have been previous concerns or there are obvious signs that the situation is escalating quickly, they may suggest a referral to a paediatrician (a children's medical specialist).

The general practitioner may also suggest seeing a psychologist. They may develop a mental health treatment plan (enabling Medicare rebates) and suggest some psychologists in the local area for you to contact for an appointment. This may take some time, and while waiting for appointments it will be important to continue to support the child. It can be helpful to keep a journal recording what is happening. You could encourage the child to keep a diary of their feelings as well, while working hard on listening and being curious about what is happening for them. All of the information in this book about building positive mental health will be relevant.

Sometimes it may be necessary to seek more intensive support than an individual psychologist can provide, and a referral may be made by the school, the general practitioner or the psychologist to a public mental health service (often called the Child and Adolescent/Youth Mental Health Service). This service usually works with children where there are considerable concerns, multiple issues, or some aspect of risk involved. There is usually a team allocated to work with the child to conduct a comprehensive assessment and treatment plan. Family support services may also prove useful when support for parenting and family issues would be helpful.

Beginning to work with a psychologist or other mental health professional

When you do meet with the psychologist, you will be asked to provide information about the child's early development as well as the family situation. There will likely be questionnaires, such as the Strengths & Difficulties Questionnaires (https://www.sdqinfo.org/), that you and the teacher will be asked to complete. Sometimes the parents have an initial session first to provide this information without the child present. This allows the parents to talk more freely than they would in front of the child. Other sessions may include a combination of the child with one or both parents or the child alone (for part of the session).

Having some questions ready for the psychologist would be helpful, such as:

- How will you work with the child (and us)?
- What role will we play in the sessions?
- What will happen if the child is reluctant to attend the session without me?
- How long would you usually see a child for?
- What can we do to support the child at home?
- How should we describe the appointments to the child?
- Are there any local supports for parents that could be helpful to us?

- How often should the sessions be?
- How will we know what to do between sessions?
- If you are concerned about the child, how will you communicate with us?
- If we are concerned between sessions, what should we do?

Seeing a psychologist for the first time may be confronting as you face many questions and come to terms with what's happening for the child and your family. Sometimes you will discover aspects of your child's life or worries that you were unaware of, and this can be difficult as you begin to learn that you can't control every aspect of a child's life or know everything about them. While we've been working to improve the stigma around mental health for decades and encouraging people to feel comfortable to seek help from psychologists and other mental health professionals, the reality is that it can still be difficult for people to do this. We may think we can handle things or at least want to try to handle things, and it's only when we reach a point where we realise that we can't that we seek help. At that point we may feel like we've failed, and seeing a mental health professional might represent that failure. This happens in the context of stigma that may still be present despite years of awareness-raising activities. To use a physical health comparison, we know that the earlier we get concerns checked out, the more likely we are to catch things before they get worse, giving us more options for treatment and often helping us to feel better because we have done something about the problem. The same can apply with mental health concerns.

Digital technology can also play a role in supporting children's mental health, and it's useful to know what's available. A government-funded website, Our Australian e-Mental Health Directory (https://www.emhprac.org.au/directory/?service_target=child-and-youth-services), provides a directory of online programs and resources available for children and young people. Sometimes these programs can be useful alongside seeing a mental health professional, and sometimes they can be useful as standalone programs. Exploring what's available is a good idea as another option for gaining support.

Working in partnership with your psychologist or mental health professional

Each mental health professional will have their own approach to the way they work with you. I can speak best about the way that psychologists typically work, so I'll outline this to give you an idea of what to expect. For primary school-aged children, parents will need to give informed consent to assessment and treatment. Parents will often be quite involved in the sessions, particularly for younger children. The psychologist is likely to spend a fair bit of time gathering information from you and your child. They might want to see you as a family as well as individually. Even though you will be heavily involved, it is also important for the psychologist to see the child without parents and for confidentiality to be assured so that the child feels comfortable sharing information. The psychologist might also ask permission to speak to the child's school. This may take some time, and it can be frustrating when we want answers to our concerns and yet the psychologist just seems to be asking more and more questions. It can take a few sessions also for people to feel comfortable talking openly with the psychologist – what we might call the building of rapport. This relates to trust and may also reflect our unfamiliarity with sharing reflections on our lives, our thoughts and our feelings. Of course, if there are immediate safety concerns, the psychologist will focus on those and work with parents to prioritise safety, which could include developing a safety plan together. The psychologist will raise any concerns with you. For longer-term support, however, more information is needed. The psychologist may be working towards gathering information for what is called a "case formulation". This is an approach that brings together the training and skills of the psychologist with the information you provide across the following areas:

1. **Presenting problem** – current key concern or problem that brought you to see the psychologist (which may not end up being the actual concern or problem)
2. **Predisposing factors** – vulnerabilities or factors that predispose the person to develop the problem
3. **Precipitating factors** – stressors or triggers that have impacted to lead to the problem at this time
4. **Perpetuating factors** – maintaining factors that keep the problem occurring
5. **Positive factors** – strengths and capacities that can be built on to help resolve the situation.

Through gathering this information in a systematic way, the psychologist can develop with you and your child a hypothesis about what is happening at the moment, what factors might have contributed to this situation arising at this time, and what will therefore be the best way forward to resolve the situation. Hopefully, through this process you and your child can gain a better understanding of what is going on and what might have contributed to it. There's likely to be more than one perspective, with each of you bringing different aspects to the way you see the situation. It helps to understand the family as a dynamic, where the experiences or behaviour of one family member impacts on the others, and to also recognise the impact of factors outside of the individual child and family, such as school and peers.

Importantly, the idea is not to lay blame or use the information to criticise anyone but to really understand what is happening so that the way forward will be clearer and any efforts to improve the situation will be realistic and can be sustained over time. Rushing too quickly into solutions may mean that important underlying factors are overlooked and simplistic responses are developed that lead to a rebounding of problems later. For some people, that can mean jumping from crisis to crisis. It is important to trust the process and recognise that the situation took time to develop, so will take time to resolve. Focusing on small steps or goals and recognising efforts and achievements will help you feel like progress is being made.

The psychologist might also ask you to complete a family genogram. This can be a time-effective way for the psychologist to get a sense of the family, family history, relationships between members, and historical factors which might form part of the predisposing factors mentioned above. Sometimes we aren't aware that there are family values, beliefs and experiences that flow through generations and can lead to patterns of behaviour that we take for granted. This is especially the case for traumatic experiences, which impact on the way we see the world and our role within it. We all have blind spots and see some of the ways we do things as normal because it's the way our family has always been. Having a psychologist explore this with us can help these become illuminated. Once we recognise these, we can start to understand some of the unspoken rules and ways of doing things that might be contributing to challenges for us.

Once the assessment has been completed, the psychologist may provide you with an overview of how things seem to them. This is a chance for you and your child to let the psychologist know what makes sense to you, or whether there are other things you think need to be factored in, or whether some things have been given too much weight. Ideally this is a collaborative process where you work together to make sense of what is going on. Sometimes this can be challenging. We all have things in our lives that we prefer not to think about or whose importance we diminish. Similarly, there might be strengths or positives that are overlooked or disregarded. Being open and ready to hear and trust what the psychologist – as a skilled practitioner who is external to the situation – has to say will help you to face the reality of what is happening. It's only from that position that you can move forward and develop plans that will be useful.

Developing a plan with the psychologist or other mental health professional

Depending on the way the psychologist works, this discussion might include a diagnosis or provisional diagnosis, such as anxiety. If so, they might then propose a treatment plan based on the current evidence about what has been shown through research to be helpful. There might be some queries about neurodiversity or other possible concerns that may require more time to explore. Concerns about safety will always be a priority. Some psychologists might be less open to a diagnosis, particularly for younger children, but may come up with a treatment plan related to the symptoms and concerns raised during the assessment period. Goals might relate to increasing self-confidence and enhancing self-awareness and social skills, as these are all aspects of a child's development that are critical to their mental health and may be impacted by the difficulties they are having.

Having a plan for you to keep in contact with the mental health professional, particularly during stressful periods, will be critical. You might find that this needs to be more frequent initially, but over time, as other supports come into place, the sessions can be reduced. Having other contact details will be important too, particularly for emergencies. Having an approach where parents work together with the child and other important people in their lives, such as school staff and extended family, will be most effective.

Types of treatments or interventions you can expect for your child

You will be guided by the mental health professional in relation to what treatment or intervention will be most helpful for your child. This intervention will initially focus on assessment and safety. The assessment process may have provided some useful information about your child's needs that can be prioritised and built into a treatment plan. Knowing what is happening and what homework tasks may be set will be important for the parent so that the responsibility can be shared. This is particularly the case for younger children, where it's unrealistic to expect a child to try new things or do things differently without the support of adults.

Research is still quite limited for a broad range of effective interventions for children's mental health problems; however, there is evidence that supports behavioural and/or cognitive behaviour therapy-based interventions (Hudson et al., 2023). These interventions would need to be tailored to meet the cognitive abilities of the child and could include parents to support the child. Typically, mental health practitioners working with primary school-aged children would use play therapy. This approach taps into children's natural interest in play, doesn't rely too much on language, and works well to engage children. The evidence base for this is continuing to grow, though it is difficult to research as it can be unstructured and child-led (rather than structured and manualised). It fits well with approaches that are respectful of the child and enable the child to have a voice in the sessions (Koukourikos et al., 2021).

Support for yourself as well as the child

You may also want to talk to the psychologist about seeking support for yourself. While the psychologist will likely be keen to see you as a key part of your child's family, remember that their primary focus will be on your child. However, they will be able to recommend colleagues who can see you for your own support. It's important that these sessions are kept separate, so that you can all have the opportunity to talk openly and freely about how things are going for you. While it is hoped that the experience of partnering with a mental health professional to support your child will be a positive and respectful process, it may also lead parents to question themselves and their role. It may trigger past experiences or memories from their own childhood. If their own childhood has been difficult, they may be reminded of some of those experiences or have a range of emotions about how this is playing out now in their current family. Having a place to talk about this aspect of their parenting can be helpful and a good opportunity to address some of those concerns as well as being a springboard for learning more about themselves. For some parents, seeking help for their child is a first step that helps them to think about what the child needs that may be separate from their own needs or experience and can be seen as a positive way to support their child in the here and now.

This early experience of help-seeking can play an important role in children's willingness to seek help in the future and to feel hopeful that there will always be people who can help them. Your modelling of the importance of help-seeking will help them to see that it is a healthy approach to understanding and caring for themselves.

REFLECTIVE QUESTIONS

- What thoughts do you have about children and mental health difficulties?
- How would you feel about approaching a mental health professional for support for your child?
- What signs would you be most likely to notice that suggest a mental health difficulty in your child?
- What signs might be less obvious to you?
- What might get in the way of seeking professional mental health support for your child?
- Who can support you in making decisions about the need for seeking help for your child's mental health?
- Where would be the best places to start to seek help?
- What questions would you need answered if talking to a mental health professional about support for your child?
- If you have sought mental health support previously, what helped you most?
- How do you view your role in supporting a child with mental health difficulties?
- How would you feel about seeking support from a mental health professional for yourself as well as your child?

CHAPTER 10

Parents caring for themselves

Right from the moment we learn that we are having a baby, we begin, consciously and unconsciously, the process of setting expectations for them, and for ourselves as parents. These beliefs or expectations are often reinforced by people around us. For some of us, these expectations may have begun to develop early in our life, perhaps in our own childhood, and certainly well before the pregnancy. These are typically big-picture, high expectations, like "I want my child to be happy and healthy". We expect that we will be the best parents, somehow not falling into the traps other parents fall into. It's easy to be critical of others, of course, and while these expectations may have been worthy expectations or hopes, they are inevitably impossible to achieve.

Once we find ourselves at home with the baby, we begin to see just how challenging day-to-day survival with a new baby can be. We may start to see the slippage. We may start to think about things we never thought about before, particularly related to the safety and wellbeing of the baby. Different expectations of ourselves and others can start to impact as we make assumptions and find others challenging them. Some of us learn to quickly adjust our expectations and find a way to become the good-enough parent, while others struggle to reconcile the mismatch between the ideal and the reality. Buying into media or celebrity representations of the perfect parent can add fuel to this challenge. With the advent of social media and often-idealised images, we can become increasingly discontented and feel like we're not able to live up to our or others' expectations. This feeling of not being good enough might be nothing new. Some of us have already held high expectations of ourselves in other areas of our lives, like how we look or what we achieve. In that case, we can just add parenting to the mix of things we wish we could do better.

It's clear that parents will be able to support their child's mental health best when they are also caring for their own. Parenting brings with it a wide variety of different experiences, some of which are enjoyable and rewarding and others stressful and demanding. When you are worried about your child's mental health, the stress will build and you can easily become overwhelmed. This can trigger off a response in your child that can distress them, and the cycle continues. Seeing their child distressed can trigger memories of parents' own previous struggles, and fears can escalate in response to that. If you or other family members have mental health problems, it may be difficult to get that out of your mind, and you may be stuck with the worry that this will happen to your child as well. All these thoughts and feelings can impact on how you respond to your child.

What can parents caring for themselves look like?

One of the biggest challenges for parents can be maintaining their own interests and identity. Giving themselves permission to do things just for themselves when their children seem so needy can be challenging. Parents can receive a lot of messages about what a "good parent" does or doesn't do. Often we see images or stories of parents being there for their kids, but what is often missing from these images or stories is how parents can only continue to be there for their kids if they have their own self-care mechanisms in place. Parents can't keep giving when they are, to use a car analogy, running on empty. They need to refuel on a regular basis and they need to use fuel of a sufficient quality to make sure the engine runs well. Not having time for themselves, or only snatching a few moments to do something for themselves here and there, rather than having this time built into their lives, is likely to lead to both physical and mental health risks. Sometimes when I worked with parents in groups, this was one of the most important learnings for the participants. Sometimes they had neglected their own basic health needs. For example, some of them decided to have a physical health check-up after realising that they had spent so much time caring for their kids that they'd neglected their own basic health maintenance. At times, this did reveal underlying health issues that had been glossed over as tiredness. Others recognised the need to invest in their relationships with other adults, including partners, particularly if worrying about the child had led to conflicts or a disconnection. This often meant giving themselves permission to prioritise spending solid of blocks of time with adults without the kids. Sometimes, when they had really gelled, the group participants continued to spend time together socially and support each other after the formal sessions ended.

Prioritising time for self-care

Prioritising time for yourself often requires communicating this to others, perhaps to seek their support to enable this to occur. Feeling confident enough to have this conversation can be a challenge, particularly if this is the first time this has been discussed. It can be helpful to identify times when you have felt worn out or haven't been as fully present as you could have been. Noticing the various ways you spend your time in a day – time divided between yourself and others – can help to build a case for focusing on time for yourself. If you think about both the physical and emotional demands on your time, you will gain a sense of how demanding being a parent can be.

If you recognise that it's easy for your needs to be lost when caring for others, you will be able to see the lack of balance that can sometimes creep in. Ideally, we should all have some time to ourselves, some busy times, and some time with others. This simple idea can help us to notice when our time is being skewed and other aspects of our lives are being affected. It will help if you convince yourself first that spending time caring for yourself is important before you talk to anyone else about it, although finding a supportive person to discuss it with first could help you to identify the ways that a lack of self-care is impacting on you.

Signs that you need to prioritise yourself more

Some of the signs you could look out for are:

- **Physical illness** – particularly immune system problems, like getting lots of colds, feelings of exhaustion, stomach upsets, headaches, and aches and pains as muscles tense up.

- **Changes in appetite and sleep patterns** – more or less than usual.

- **Episodes of shallow breathing** – feelings of panic.

- **Tiredness** – perhaps because your sleep is disrupted or your diet is missing some key nutrients.

- **Mind wandering, racing thoughts or confusion** – having so many thoughts that you can't concentrate on any one thing at a time, feeling overwhelmed or fixated on worries. This can lead to a lack of confidence and inability to make decisions.

- **Misunderstandings or misinterpretations** – may be caused by not fully tuning in or understanding what the other person is saying. Can lead to conflicts.

- **Agitation, lack of patience or irritability** – could be related to all the above.

Catching signs of stress early

You may know yourself well enough to know which of these signs, or other symptoms, are most likely to affect you. They are the same signs that a person experiencing burnout in a workplace could feel, and if not dealt with well can build up over time and lead to mental health problems as well as physical health issues. As with other aspects of our lives, there may be times when priorities shift and we need to focus on one aspect over others. For example, when a child is unwell our focus can shift to their needs and our own needs might be less of a focus. If this continues beyond the period of need, the habit of not noticing our own needs can creep in and an imbalance between needs can be created and continue without us noticing. Balancing time caring for your child and time for yourself means seeking out opportunities to regularly do small things that help you feel like you are taking back some control of your life and prioritising your own needs when you can. They don't have to be big things, just small things that mark the moment and tell yourself and others that you are important. This is where allowing others to care for you can give you the space to do something for yourself. You'll notice that taking some time for yourself can help you to process your thoughts and feelings so that you can gain a different perspective.

Discovering small ways to care for yourself

Examples of small ways to care for yourself include:

- Having a bubble bath or shower before bed.
- Reading a book for half an hour instead of doing household tasks.
- Writing a journal – writing a small amount each day can become a habit where feelings and thoughts can be expressed. You can use a physical diary or set up a space on your mobile phone or tablet. You can find apps that will provide you with prompts and reminders to help to build this into your day.

- Keep a "gratitude diary" – writing three things you are grateful for every morning can help your day start off positively and give you a focus. You could also, or instead, do this at night to help you to reflect on the day.
- Plan to take a course or start or revisit a hobby now or when you have more time – break the planning down into steps and relish the opportunity to look forward to doing something you will enjoy.
- Make time for a coffee catch-up with a friend you haven't seen for a while (or make an appointment to Zoom or FaceTime if they're not physically close by).
- Identify one night each week when you prioritise your own time. It could be a television show you like or an interest that you want to pursue. You may need to plan ahead and get some support to make this happen. Perhaps begin with one night a month and build on it when you can. Similarly, you could do this to spend time with a partner or other important people in your life.

Learning to be self-compassionate

It's easy as a parent to take on feelings of self-blame and criticise yourself, particularly when things don't seem to be going well for your child. People can often be more critical of themselves than they would be of another person. Perhaps they have set themselves high expectations and find it difficult to live up to those expectations every day. Perhaps they have been able to do well in other areas of their lives and then find it difficult when parenting proves more challenging. Perhaps they feel criticised by others, whether this is real or imagined. Sometimes, comparing yourself with what you see on social media or how others seem to be dealing with parenting can lead to unfair self-criticism.

Self-compassion has risen in popularity in recent years, with a number of authors highlighting the benefits. Dr Kristin Neff (https://self-compassion.org/) is a researcher and author who first published her book *Self-Compassion* in 2011. Since then, she has updated her work, taking new challenges such as Covid-19 into account. She describes self-compassion as treating ourselves with the same warmth, care, and concern that we'd naturally show to a good friend. She reports that recent research has found that self-compassionate people were better able to cope with the challenges of Covid-19, they were less fearful and lonely, more satisfied with their lives, and could parent their children effectively, despite the stress of working and schooling from home. In her chapter about self-compassionate parenting she describes the value of teaching children to have self-compassion to help them deal with the "inevitable pain and imperfection of life" (Neff, 2021, p. 207). She also describes the benefits of being self-compassionate as a parent for children, who learn from their parents' modelling of what it means to be compassionate to oneself and others.

Self-compassion requires us to recognise our own suffering. This means stopping or slowing in order to recognise our suffering and acknowledge how hard it is. If the suffering comes from self-judgement, it can be harder to see that as moments of suffering. A focus on independence and individual achievement can work against compassionately seeing ourselves and our mistakes. Sometimes people resist the idea of self-compassion because they see it as self-pity or over-indulgence. Self-compassion, instead, should be seen as critical to health and wellbeing and can actually lead to proactive behaviour to better oneself. Self-compassion can help us to learn and grow from mistakes and over time to let go of perfectionism and work towards achieving emotional wellbeing and contentment. It allows us to tap into our strengths and capacities, become more open to the imperfect human condition, and accordingly start to feel more secure, accepted and alive. Being self-compassionate can therefore help us to cope with life as a parent and to provide a model to children to break generational patterns of self-criticism and perfectionism.

So what does self-compassion look like in day-to-day life? If we focus on dealing with difficult emotions, self-compassion provides three doorways to help:

1. You can give yourself kindness and care.
2. You can remind yourself that encountering pain is part of the shared human experience.
3. You can hold your thoughts and emotions in mindful awareness.

The parenting experience and feelings of shame and guilt

It's clear that the groundwork is laid early in their parenting lives for parents to blame themselves and take on shame and guilt when things don't go right with their kids. Having a child will tap right into these feelings of not being good enough and lead to parents feeling shame and guilt. It's no wonder, then, that parents of children who are experiencing mental health difficulties will even more easily blame themselves and experience shame and embarrassment. This can serve to shut them down and stop them talking to others and even prevent them from reaching out to get help. Overcoming shame can be challenging, but talking to other parents in a similar situation can be one of the most helpful ways to reduce these feelings and gain self-acceptance and confidence in our abilities again. It can be helpful to know that feelings of shame and guilt are all about the things that matter to us. They can also be about the expectations of others about what should be done or not done.

Shame is often considered to be more about ourselves, whereas guilt is about things in the world, such as perceived failures and events that we feel responsibility for. A person who feels guilty regrets something they've done, while someone who feels shame regrets something about themselves as a person. Feelings of shame go deeper to a sense of self and identity. Guilt can more easily be resolved by acting to repair the situation, if possible, whereas feelings of shame can become personalised and more difficult to shift.

Feelings of shame attached to a child's mental health problems can tap into earlier times parents have felt shame, even as a child themselves. It's helpful to recognise this so that you can understand why you may be experiencing strong feelings or different feelings from usual. Parents all bring their unique life experiences to their parenting, and guilt and shame are examples of how parenting a child with mental health difficulties can remind them of earlier experiences. If you think about parenting a child with mental health difficulties, there may not be one issue that you feel guilty or shameful about that can easily be fixed. It is possible that you will feel guilty and potentially shameful about your parenting as a whole and the child will feel guilty and potentially shameful about what they have been doing or not doing, particularly if they are aware of the impact on others. In such cases, apologising to each other might open the door to being able to get along together and agreeing to be honest and open. This might take time, and you may need professional support to help guide the conversation towards one of respect, shared responsibilities, and hope for the future.

Recognising and coping with fears as a parent

Parents may have many fears about their children's wellbeing. These fears may be real or inflated. Over the course of their lives, and their children's lives, these fears change. From the birth of their children, parents worry about their very survival, feeling the burden, along with the joy, of being totally responsible for them and keeping them alive. As their children grow, parents learn to adjust, and what they worried about the year before may no longer be thought about. Those fears will be replaced by new ones as children's worlds open and they gradually let go of their parents' hold. While parents may learn to adjust and cope better, each new stage of childhood towards adolescence opens a whole new range of fears and anxieties that parents often haven't dared think about before. Some of those fears might relate to memories of their own childhood and teenage years. Sometimes fears come from hearing stories in the media or from other parents who have been there before them. Often the scary stories are told rather than the more calming stories of normal day-to-day life with children. Just as people are primed to feel guilty, they also are primed to feel scared as parents.

When people feel fear, their body and mind respond in ways that can leave them feeling out of control. They might experience panic or a numbing of thoughts and feelings. They might have a physical response where they feel sick. Their thinking process might slow down, and they may not be able to find the words they need. Their vigilant brain might over-think and jump to conclusions that increase the fears – and the cycle begins over again. It can be a debilitating experience and one that can lead to feelings of incompetence. The fear may push them away from their children. At the very time children need their parents most, the fear might make the parents so anxious that they become judgmental or blaming. The fear might also make them want to shut down, shut the children away from them, or shut themselves away from their support networks. Their thoughts and feelings might become silenced as they struggle to contain them, at the very time when they need their thoughts and feelings to be clear, to help them work out what matters and guide them to prioritising those things.

Being a witness to the struggle of a child who is experiencing mental health difficulties can be frightening and traumatic for parents. It can create a cycle of negative thoughts and emotions that impact on functioning and wellbeing. They may want to protect others from knowing the extent of their experience, so they may try to deal with their feelings on their own. Their day-to-day routine may have been shattered as they now face their number one worry about helping their child feel better. When people feel fear, they are likely to become hypervigilant. This creates a physiological impact where they are jumpy and on edge. This state of high energy is not sustainable over time without leading to burnout. It can mean that they are so worried about their kids that they tend to over-parent – both the child they are worried about but also other kids or people they care about. They may start to see things through a narrow lens of risk and worry about things more than they used to – and potentially much more than they need to. They may start to lose perspective on what are real worries or risks, and this can have a negative impact on others.

Understanding the way that fear triggers a physical response can be helpful. If you know that thoughts of fear and worry can lead to a particular feeling that in turn sets off a particular behaviour, you can begin to focus on reducing the impact of those thoughts. You can try to find ways to give yourself a break from the fear. This might be by distracting yourself, even for a few minutes at a time where you give yourself permission to not think about the worry. You might need to actively turn off your phone for a few minutes or go for a short walk without it. You could try some positive self-talk where you tell yourself that your child is OK and you can relax. You could share your thoughts and gain support by sharing the responsibility. This needs to start off with small efforts and build up over time. You should remember that feelings of fear are important because they tell you a lot about what you value and what or who matters most to you. They also play a protective role in helping you to be alert and keep safe. You can't entirely dismiss them, of course, and most likely don't want to, but you can certainly learn to put them into perspective and not let them rule your life.

Keeping up with our social connections

Like children, parents are social beings. Being alone with a problem makes it harder to bear. When parenting, people become so close to the situation that it's pretty much impossible to be totally objective. Seeking help can mean connecting with others who have been through or are going through a similar experience. Parenting programs can sometimes become sources of mutual support. Often, when parents get together in a formal, structured setting, they are able to experience being with other parents in a safe space to share their experiences, admit their feelings without fear of judgement, and explore together the way forward. As a facilitator of these groups, I often noticed that the essence of the work was in the way these parents supported each other, not from any remarkable skills or insight I was passing on. It was their social need to connect, to be with others, to feel understood and heard, that was valued. This often gave them the strength to return home with some degree of renewed hope. I came to believe that my job in these groups was to set up an environment that could be hope-giving, that could enable the parents to feel understood and to have the courage to face another day with their children. It strikes me now that this is exactly what parents are trying to do with their children.

Parental self-care as an act of care for children

Parents can't support a child who is struggling with their mental health all on their own. They need some space to reflect on their own experience, time to do some things they enjoy and keep a sense of containment in our lives. Having a child who is struggling will cause a range of responses from the parent, and having some time to process those responses and accompanying feelings is essential for parents to be able to sustain themselves and their relationship with the child. The child will also benefit from feeling that there is a support team around them, rather than a heavy reliance on one person. This can be a testing time, with the relationship with the child becoming more intense and focused. It can be an opportunity to focus on what is most important, what really matters to us, and what we might be able to do to better understand each other and continue to work on strengthening our relationship. Bringing our full selves as parents to the relationship means having some time to remind ourselves of who we are and what we need, to be able to be the parent we want to be in this situation. This takes time and the opportunity to notice and reflect.

Building your village of people who support you and your family

Parents shouldn't let themselves feel like they are the only ones holding this together. You might find it helpful to grab a piece of paper and reflect on the village around your family. Think about the people who support you and your family. Begin to make a list and then take a look at it to see what you notice:

- Who are the people you can talk to easily about your worries?
- Who are the people who won't judge?
- Who won't give you simplistic solutions?
- Who are the people who will listen to you and be there for you regardless of what the problem is?
- Who is better at providing practical rather than emotional support?

As you think critically about the people on your list, you might begin to cross some people off. Some people might not easily understand this particular situation or will want to help you so much that they will jump in and try to solve the problem for you. Some just won't be able to see your perspective. You might like to move those people to a different list. Those people can still be supportive and fun to be with, but they're not the people you know you can rely on at the most critical times in your parenting role.

You might be able to think about people who have been through their own battles with their kids' or their own mental health. They might work with children or have a good understanding of the situations parents and children find themselves in. These are the people who will be most able to listen to you and also make some suggestions when you are ready to hear them. Be careful, though, that they don't tell you what you should do. Remember that every situation can be different and work out what you need to do in your unique situation.

You might be looking at your list and thinking you don't have anyone you are confident can be there for you at this time. You may have friends with younger kids who just won't understand what's happening for you – and you mightn't want to scare them with your worries and experiences. Your friends might be from your workplace, and you might like to keep your home and work lives separate. It can be helpful for you to have a space away from the concerns of home. There may also be someone who is going through a similar struggle to you, but you're not reaching out to each other. Your family members may not be physically close to you but may want to help in whatever ways they can once they know what's happening for you. Try to take a broad view in looking at your possible support network and think about how you might be able to test the waters by reaching out and seeing how people respond. Bear in mind that there may be people who would like to help if they knew what you need. Be mindful also that it can be difficult to ask for help, especially if you are usually independent and capable of managing situations on your own. Just as we would say to our children that reaching out for help is a strength, it can be helpful to remind ourselves that this is the case for us too and provides good modelling to children.

Help-seeking as an act of self-care

If, after doing this activity, you feel that there are not enough people around you and your child, you might consider seeking out further support. There are various ways to do this. There are online forums that you can reach out to. Take a look at the list in the resources section and explore the websites to get a sense of whether they suit you. Your general practitioner might be a useful support, but bear in mind that although they are often the first port of call, they aren't all experienced with providing support to families and children with mental health difficulties. Check to see if there are any general practitioners in your area who specialise in mental health and working with children and families. They will most likely have undertaken some additional training and will be more likely to know some local services that can help you.

Bear in mind that there are at least two sides of the helping equation. Your partner and/or other family members will also benefit from support during this time, and you will no doubt find yourself being a support for them. You will need some help and support for yourself as a parent to support your child but also as a person to keep yourself healthy and coping with your life. Family members can help each other, but having support from someone outside of the situation can be helpful to gain some perspective. It can take time to find the most useful help at any point in time. If you've had a good experience in the past, it can be worth revisiting that if possible or identifying what was helpful. It's important to be ready to seek help in order for it to be useful. Recognising help-seeking as a strength rather than a vulnerability will help you feel more comfortable and engage more fully.

Seeking professional mental health support

If you are feeling concerned and becoming overwhelmed, it may be useful for you to see your own mental health professional to provide you with a safe space to talk through these concerns and feelings. You will need to see someone who hasn't seen your child, as there needs to be separation in roles. You could ask your child's mental health professional for suggestions for someone who could help you. This is often a good place to start and can help you feel confident that the person will be a good fit for you. This may be easier than trying to find someone and ringing someone cold. Sometimes, though, it's necessary to search, and the Find a Psychologist website (https://psychology.org.au/find-a-psychologist) is a good starting point.

You may decide to let your child know that you are going to see someone or you may choose to keep this private, particularly if you are not sure how your child will react. You should be careful not to make it sound like the child's experience is all about you. They will be focused on their own needs and feelings and will want those validated rather than hearing about how their behaviour is affecting you or causing you distress. Even though they may not say it, they may be well aware of the effect on you and could be feeling guilty about it. If you do choose to let your child know that you are seeking help, you are modelling good self-care, and this might be helpful in normalising help-seeking. It's therefore important to think through what to share, how to frame it, and when will be the best time to share this information.

During sessions with a mental health professional, you may explore how you are feeling and responding to the situation. You may also get some help in coming up with some ideas about what else you might be able to do to support your child. They obviously won't know exactly what is going on for your child, so they will want to focus on how you are responding and feeling, rather than providing specific advice about what your child needs. For some parents, this support can provide them with a way to manage their emotions and worries so that they are better equipped to continue to support their child. This might help with self-awareness about how their own experience and behaviour can play out and impact on the child. It might also mean that they feel calmer when having conversations with their child and more able to broach what are difficult discussions about mental health concerns.

Seeing a mental health professional might also help you understand the experience of getting professional support and how to encourage your child to do so. You might be able to gain a perspective of what it is like to go through this process, as well as what is difficult about seeking help. Taking the time to focus on yourself can help you to consider all the other aspects of your life that may be impacted by your child's current situation. It can help you to gain perspective on the effects on your other children, your partner, extended family, friends and work. You might find the opportunity to problem-solve ways to manage each of these situations rather than rely on your usual ways that may or may not be helpful in the uniqueness of this situation.

Accessing professional support can help you to challenge some of your long-held beliefs about yourself and your role as parent. It can help to give you permission to focus on yourself and prioritise what is most important at that point in time. This might mean reducing some of your usual commitments for a period of time. The mental health professional might also help you to tackle your greatest fears, particularly the worry about your child being distressed. These are not easy to face, and that's why it's so important to find a mental health professional that you can connect with well and trust. Sometimes parents don't realise how their feelings are showing to others or affecting what they say and do. You might also find that you can talk through any feelings of responsibility, guilt and shame that are arising for you. Putting names to these feelings can help to normalise them and defuse their power. Looking at your role as a parent, its limitations, and the strengths and capacities you have can be affirming while helping you to be realistic about what you can and cannot do.

REFLECTIVE QUESTIONS

- What do you do already for your own self-care?
- What kinds of self-care are most difficult to fit into your current life?
- What messages do you receive about self-care?
- Who supports (or could support) you in being able to care for yourself?
- What acts of self-care are most meaningful for you?
- What does self-care mean to you?
- How compassionate are you towards yourself?
- What difficulties do you face in your parenting life?
- What bothers you most as a parent?
- What gets in the way of your self-care?
- What would be a first step you could make to enhance your self-care?
- How do you feel about seeking professional help for yourself?

CHAPTER 11

What can parents do to build hope in themselves and their kids?

Exploring all of the aspects of our lives and those of our children that can be concerning can remind us of the importance of finding ways to create hopefulness to face the challenges and to be able to enjoy life. Understanding how children see the world is an important part of this to prevent our adult assumptions from overriding what might be happening for them. It can be easy for adults to think they know what is happening for their children and what they need. However, in my work I notice the gap that can arise when parents make assumptions like this. I see it when parents talk and children sit and hear what their parents are saying about them. When I invite the child to talk about what it's like for them or what else is happening that perhaps their parents don't know about, the door can open for parents to hear a whole lot of experiences they weren't aware of – and couldn't possibly know about.

Children have their own experience of life that adults can't fully comprehend. Their experience in the family might be witnessed by others, but what it feels like for the child can't be fully understood just by watching. For example, when a child attends a day at school, they have hundreds of interactions with other students, teachers and other adults. Some of these interactions will be minor and unmemorable, but other interactions may be impactful. Asking children how their day was may or may not provide them with an opportunity to share these experiences. Some children will more openly share details about their feelings and experiences, while other children will be more closed. This might relate to their temperament, their stage of development, their language abilities, and even the type of experience they have had. Some experiences can be hard to share, particularly if the child feels overly responsible, embarrassed, or worried that they'll be in trouble.

This means that our hope-creating as parents needs to take into account four different aspects:

1. Make sense first for ourselves.
2. Listen carefully to children.
3. Explore together.
4. Problem-solve.

Make sense first for ourselves

When tackling challenging situations for ourselves and with children, we may tend to be reactive or jump to conclusions, perhaps repeating patterns from the past and doing what we always do. New issues that now face us require us to think about these in new ways, gather information, and talk with others to help make sense of what is happening. Understanding this for ourselves before we talk with children or try to resolve the situation will help us to feel more confident and be more clear in our communication with children. Children will benefit from having adults who are able to help them feel confident. It helps children to see their parents coping and having plans for how to deal with situations they face. This will be particularly helpful during times of uncertainty or as we face new situations.

Sometimes we might need to think in the moment about something that is happening or in response to what children say or ask us. This might make it difficult to come up with a satisfactory answer in the short time frame available. It might be better to buy some time to go away, find out more, and take the time to reflect. We do this as psychologists in our work – we call it reflection-in-action and reflection-on-action. Reflecting in action is when we reflect as something is happening – we consider the situation, decide how to act, and act immediately. Sometimes this is necessary and the best thing to do. When we face bigger issues or challenges, however, it can be useful to reflect on action. This is when we reflect after something has happened. We might reconsider the situation with the benefit of some space and hindsight and think about what needs changing for the future. This approach was originally developed in the 1990s by Donald Schön, a philosopher. Since then, many researchers have refined the model and expanded it to incorporate feelings and evaluation as well as actions. Most recent research has focused on a four-dimensional model which adds reflection-before-action and reflection-beyond action (e.g., Edwards, 2017). These ideas of reflective practice, although designed for use by health and education professionals, could also be very useful for parents during times of uncertainty, helping them build confidence and respond in ways that feel thought-through rather than reactive.

Listen carefully to children

I see the gap in parents' understanding of their children's experiences when I provide children and their parents with the opportunity to complete screening tools related to the child's mental health. It's usual that the child will score more highly on mental health problems than the parents. This is also seen in research studies. In fact, it's now become so evident that researchers are calling for efforts to be made to better include children in research so that we aren't just relying on adults' views about how they are. This has been a long-standing concern, and I came across it when I was undertaking my doctoral research over 15 years ago with teenagers with intellectual disabilities, a group who are not often included in research. I used a methodology called Photovoice to ensure that these teenagers could be included. As the name suggests, Photovoice uses photos to show how the person is experiencing their life. It can then be accompanied by interviews and focus groups to explore the themes that emerge. This methodology has also been used with children and provides us with opportunities to really tune in to the child's world as they see it. Just as we might ask a child to draw a picture to show us what's happening, it removes some of the barriers of language that can be restrictive when children try to explain new things.

While I'm not suggesting that parents should necessarily use Photovoice to learn more about their child's experiences, I do think adults need to work hard on finding ways to better hear children's experiences. In order to listen well to children, adults need to have an open attitude and be willing to put aside their own assumptions and views about what might be happening for the child. If you think about people you go to when you want to talk through a problem or experience, you'll probably notice that they:

- are likely to listen without judgement
- allow you the time to talk through how you feel without jumping to conclusions or solutions
- validate your feelings as legitimate and real
- ask curious questions to help you explore your feelings and experiences at a deeper level
- allow silence for processing of feelings, particularly if they are strong and uncomfortable
- ask what you would like from them or if there is anything they can do to help.

This approach might seem obvious when you think about listening to another adult, but rarely would it be the way adults think about listening to children. It's worth taking a moment to think about the differences. Perhaps we think that children aren't capable of talking through their feelings and coming up with their own solutions. Perhaps we think our job as adults is to take away children's problems and solve them for them. Perhaps we don't feel that the time it takes to listen and talk through feelings is necessary for children. Perhaps we aren't comfortable with seeing our children struggle, so move quickly into trying to fix their problems and make them feel better. The problem with all of these responses is that we rob children of the opportunity to learn how to express themselves, how to work through feelings and come up with solutions if they can, involving you in developing those solutions as necessary. If adults try to fix children's problems before they have listened and fully understood what the problem is, they might not be solving the problem at all or even know what the real problem is. Perhaps the child isn't really seeking a solution but just wants the comfort of being heard.

As a psychologist, one of my key skills is to listen without judgement. It requires me to switch off my own thoughts for a while and tune into what the person is saying. I need to focus on their body language, their tone of voice, their facial expressions, and what they are saying. In fact, often what I am really listening for is what they are *not* saying, what is being covered up or can't be expressed by words. I ask curious questions to help the person explore areas that they haven't been consciously aware of, or if aware, have pushed away in efforts to avoid any discomfort or pain. This takes trust and time. Sometimes it flows smoothly and at other times it can feel awkward. It's a core starting point to my work, though. How else can I understand what is happening for the person and work out with them what they need when they see me? While this also applies to my work with children, there are some key differences. Firstly, I have had some information from parents or teachers that gives me some context for the situation the child and family are facing. This can often be helpful, but I need to take care that it doesn't skew my perspective too much. By hearing from the child, I get the chance to fill in some gaps or to more deeply understand the experience from the child's point of view. While there may be some elements that are similar between the adults' version and the child's, there are often features that are missing from the adults'. Sometimes these may seem small and quite unimportant, but allowing the child to be heard may be necessary in order for adults to better make sense of what's really happening for the child and to work out how they can best help the child. Sometimes through the process of listening to children much bigger concerns are identified, and parents may be quite surprised that they have missed something that seems so obvious later but was completely obscured, perhaps in the busyness of life or because the child had hidden it so well.

Listening to children may be one of the most valuable things that adults can do. It helps the child feel valued and supported. It ensures that the child feels safe and secure in being able to share how they are feeling and what is going on for them. Importantly, it helps the child to feel less alone in their experience of life. So, what does it take to really listen to a child?

Setting up a regular listening time as part of the daily routine can be helpful. Depending on the family's routine, this could be at the end of the school day, after dinner, or at bedtime. Bedtime can be a good time but may be problematic if a worry is identified and needs time to be talked through and resolved. Some curious, open-ended questions that are positive and adjusted to the child's stage of development can help to start the conversation:

- What was the most interesting thing that happened today?
- Were all your friends at school today?
- Was there anything unusual or different about today?
- What was something that you learned today?
- What was the biggest challenge you faced?
- How did you manage the tricky parts of the day?

Having this as a daily routine can be calming for children and help them to feel supported, knowing that there will be a time when adults will be there to listen. The child will need to know that they can trust you to share anything problematic. If they think you will become upset or angry with them if they share something that was a problem, they are less likely to share it with you. If they become upset, they will need adults who can help them to manage their feelings and co-regulate. This means that adults need to be aware of their own feelings and responses. Staying present in the moment and supporting the child is critical. It can help for parents to remind themselves that the focus here should be on the child, and any feelings that arise for themselves can be dealt with separately. Sometimes children will share things that make parents angry or disappointed. These can be strong feelings that the parents will need to deal with, but at the point of sharing it is most helpful if the focus is on keeping the child talking and thanking them for sharing what may have been very difficult to share. It can help to place some boundaries around what needs to be dealt with in the moment and what might need to be talked about again. This can be good modelling for children – showing that sometimes we need to take more time to think through a worry so that we don't overreact or come up with a rushed plan about how to deal with something.

At other times the child may need us to listen, but this may not be obvious to the parent or may not fit into the scheduled time. The child's body language or behaviour might suggest there is a problem. Sometimes it's tempting to focus on the behaviour, and while there may be a need to point out that the behaviour isn't appropriate, it is most important to be curious about what the behaviour represents. Being curious is a good starting point at these times, as well as asking questions that help the child to know that you are aware that something is going on and you are ready to listen. Some helpful starting points are:

- It looks like something is bothering you. Would you like to talk about it?
- Sometimes when I get worried I get annoyed. I'm wondering if that's happening for you right now?
- I can see you're worrying about something. What's up?
- Has something happened today that's upset you?

- I'm ready to listen when you'd like to talk about what's going on.
- It's hard when something happens and we feel upset. Talking might help. Let me know when you're ready to talk about it.

We can't force a child to tell us what is bothering them, but we can open the door to make it easier for them to share their worries. The more we do this during times when there aren't obvious problems the easier it will be for children to trust us and feel comfortable in talking when a problem does arrive. Adults who model their own sharing of feelings and worries (in age-appropriate ways) will also help children to know that this is normal and helpful.

Explore together – taking children's worries seriously

Sometimes children will share their worries, and what seems very big to them can seem quite small to adults. At times like this it is important to stay tuned in to how the child is feeling. If the worry is minimised or ridiculed, it can stop the child from talking in the future. Acknowledging how the child is feeling is critical, despite how small the worry might seem to adults. Helping the child to gain some perspective about the problem might be useful, but not until the child feels heard and that their worry has been validated.

Once a child does share a worry, it is helpful for adults to validate the feeling and the content. This helps the child to truly feel heard and their feelings acknowledged. It's not just what they say but also the feeling that needs to be acknowledged. Sometimes that will be enough for the child to feel relieved. At other times the child will still be bothered, and the situation might need to be explored a bit more before the adult asks the child what they think needs to happen. It is important for the adult to avoid jumping into a solution. Sometimes children come up with the perfect solution that adults could never have thought of. Sometimes they need help from adults, and if that's the case, coming up with some suggestions can be useful. Helping the child make the decision as far as possible will be important. If the problem does require adult input, it can help to talk this through with the child, but ensure that the child feels as empowered as possible. Acknowledge how difficult it might have been to talk about the situation and feelings, and make sure the child is thanked for trusting you.

Problem solve – with support

Given that conflicts are normal in human relationships, you will be familiar with different approaches people use to resolve conflict. No doubt you will have a preferred approach when it comes to conflict in your own life. You will also have seen how conflicts were handled in your own family growing up. There are five main approaches to conflict (Thomas-Kilmann Model), each involving varying levels of assertiveness and cooperativeness:

1. **Avoiding** – ignoring or sidestepping the conflict, hoping it will resolve itself or dissipate (low in both assertiveness and cooperativeness)
2. **Accommodating** – taking steps to satisfy the other's concerns or demands at the expense of your own needs or desires (high in cooperativeness, low in assertiveness)
3. **Compromising** – finding an acceptable resolution that will partly, but not entirely, satisfy the concerns of all people involved (low in both cooperativeness and assertiveness)
4. **Competing** – when someone tries to satisfy their own desires at the expense of the other person (low in cooperativeness, high in assertiveness)
5. **Collaborating** – finding a solution that entirely satisfies the concerns of all involved parties (high in both cooperativeness and assertiveness).

Approaches that aim to collaborate are obviously most effective at ensuring that all needs are met. However, there may be situations where other approaches are appropriate. For example, when the conflict is minor with little consequences, you may choose to let it go or sort itself out rather than raise the issue, so avoiding might be appropriate. In a work situation where you have to undertake a task in a particular way, you might choose to accommodate or compromise.

Having a process to help resolve conflicts in collaborative ways is important to ensure that everyone is heard and that conflicts are resolved in a fair way. There are various models, some of which you may have come across in workplaces, which could be adapted for home. Here's a simple six-step conflict-resolution model based on the idea that interpersonal conflict is essentially a problem that needs to be solved. This model can work well even with young children:

1. **Define the conflict** – be specific about what the problem is. What do you want or need? What does the other person want or need? This requires listening and assertiveness skills. This step is very important, as you need to make sure you know what the actual problem is before trying to solve it.
2. **List possible solutions** – come up with a list of possible ways the problem could be solved. At this stage list all possible solutions without judgement.
3. **Test each solution** – rule the possibility in or out.
4. **Evaluate the solution** – will this work? How will it work? Can we all live with this solution?
5. **Agree on the solution and develop a plan to make it happen.**
6. **How did it work?** If there are still concerns, return to step 1 to check if you missed something the first time.

Where does self-esteem fit into hope-creating?

About 20 years ago we were hearing a lot about the importance of self-esteem. I even included a topic called "Building your child's self-esteem" in courses I ran with parents. Self-esteem related to self-confidence and a feeling of self-satisfaction. A lack of self-esteem was thought to be an underlying problem causing a lot of issues for children. High self-esteem was related to parents praising their children and not being very critical. At the time, it was seen as a bit like a panacea for parenting and a contrast to previous parenting practices where parents tended to criticise children and not be sensitive to their feelings. Then some research started to come out that questioned this idea that high self-esteem was always good for children. The research that struck me most revealed that some kids who bullied actually had high self-esteem (Salmivalli at al., 1999). Learning about this forced me to question some of the ideas that by that time were seen as positive approaches to parenting. Self-esteem is still talked about as important, and it often surprises me how these ideas can take on a life of their own and can be hard to challenge. Having high self-esteem might mean that you are confident in yourself, but you might get that confidence from harming others or by over-selling yourself. It might come at the cost of relationships and learning to care about others. Like most psychological concepts, it's not black and white, and working towards having a strong sense of self while also caring and respecting others is probably a better approach. Understanding rights and responsibilities that we all have might be a useful way to explore this.

Having a strong sense of identity (knowing who we are) and self-worth might be better ways to describe this. These ideas can still be challenged as too individualistic, too focused on the individual rather than thinking beyond our individual selves and seeing ourselves in relation to others. This is all very important to consider when children are experiencing difficulties with their mental health. Their sense of who they are and what they stand for can be shattered and lead to a lack of valuing of their lives. Feeling isolated and of no worth to anyone can be factors related to mental health problems.

Our feelings about ourselves develop over a long period of time and are obviously challenged as people say things about us that are unkind or question aspects of who we are. As parents, we will have said things to our children that they may have interpreted in this way. Sometimes giving children honest feedback or letting them know that we are unhappy with something they've done can dent their sense of self. Some children are more sensitive than others, and even feedback given in a gentle way can be taken by some children as severe criticism. It can be difficult to know how to teach children how to behave or learn important life lessons without giving them this kind of feedback. While this is not the time to ruminate about those times, it may be useful to take some time to reflect on how your child might be feeling about themselves:

- What have you heard them say about themselves? Are there patterns or times when this is most likely to happen? Has this changed recently?
- Have you ever had the sense that they were putting on a confident face when you suspected they weren't in fact very confident at all? When was that? Does it happen in some settings more than others (e.g., with friends, with grandparents)?
- Has anyone else ever commented on their self-confidence? What did they say?
- Have you noticed that how your child behaves and what they say haven't matched at times? What did you notice? What was the situation? What might this mean?
- When have you noticed them looking genuinely proud of themselves? What happened? How did others respond?

Once you have a sense of how your child might be feeling about themselves, you'll be able to understand them better. You might be tempted to heap praise on them, but that's not the answer. Praise that is given for the sake of giving it is not genuine, and children can see through it or even find it condescending. Instead, it will be better to find a way to gently open up conversations about what you have noticed and offer to help. Trying to help them claim their own voice and let you know how they are feeling and what they need will be better. If you do feel tempted to praise them (and there will be times when this is appropriate), here are some tips:

- Focus on specifics about what you like and be clear about exactly what they have done (e.g., "Thanks for taking the food out of your bedroom").

- Don't give general praise (e.g., "You've done a great job"). Instead, be specific about how their behaviour has impacted on you (e.g., "Now that your room doesn't have any food in it, I can relax and not worry that the house is dirty").
- Reflect on how their behaviour might positively affect them (e.g., "Now that your room doesn't have any food in it, I won't be worried about the house being unclean and can stop asking you about it").

You'll see that these might just be subtle shifts in how you talk to your child, but they can make a difference to how they feel about you and your relationship, as well as about themselves. We can fall into the trap of thinking they understand what we are pleased with or not, and when we are too general they can miss our point and not understand exactly what we mean.

Taking a strengths-based approach

Helping a child to recognise their strengths and capacities as well as acknowledge and accept their limitations can be helpful. Having perfectionistic ideas where the child thinks they should do everything perfectly can get in the way of feeling worthy. As parents, we can be mirrors to our kids, helping them to recognise what it is that makes them unique and ways that they help others. Watching our own self-talk can also help, ensuring that we are modelling self-acceptance and the valuing of ourselves as we are. Talking to our children about times when we have made mistakes and how we handled it can be useful. By sharing our own experiences, we are modelling how to do this.

REFLECTIVE QUESTIONS

- How do you feel about the changes in the world that you see impacting on your children?
- What is your approach to your own worries?
- As a child, what did you worry about?
- How did adults respond to your worries when you were a child?
- What's it like for you to see your child worried? Which worries bother you most?
- How easy is it for you to listen to your child?
- How well can you reflect on what is happening or has happened?
- Would it help to take some time to reflect after a situation to help understand and plan for the future?
- What do you typically do when your child has a problem?
- What happens when you ask your child curious questions about how they are feeling or how they might be able to fix a problem?
- What happens when you encourage your child to solve a problem together?

Conclusion

While writing this book, I've been reflecting on what it takes to be a parent or another adult supporting children in the complex world that we live in. I've been thinking about the access we all have to technology, and the ways in which our traditional institutions, such as schools, churches and community more generally, support families – or don't. I'm aware of the complex nature of families and how we can't assume that extended family members or people in the community will be there to provide support. All this has led me to think about the importance of parents' ability to make sense of this complexity for themselves before they can support their children.

I've also been thinking about what children bring to their relationships with parents and other adults. Children are increasingly aware of issues in the world, as parents are no longer able to protect them from information in the way that parents could in the past. Parents who deny this reality or try to protect children too much won't be in a position to open the door to good communication and may not encourage children to approach them to ask questions that provide the opportunity for parents to find out what is bothering them. Having these conversations doesn't mean not taking into account the child's age and stage of development when providing answers or supporting them. It's OK to say that we don't know when we genuinely don't know or to say that this is something we can keep talking about, with more information becoming shared as they get older. It's OK to keep some boundaries around what is shared with children, so long as we are aware that they can seek out answers for themselves if they feel that we aren't being open. Being clear about what is an adult worry and what is a child worry can be helpful. This helps the child feel safe and secure, while also having their thoughts acknowledged and validated. Perhaps feeling safe and secure is the greatest antidote against hopelessness.

Facing an uncertain world is challenging for adults, so taking some time to reflect on what our own values are, what is important to us, and talking to others about these can be helpful. Remaining hopeful takes effort, and we need to balance hope with reality in order to get through each day and find ways to manage situations we find ourselves in. Being hopeful doesn't mean ignoring what is obvious or wishing issues away. It's actually about facing the realities and finding ways to make sense of them in order to be able to respond with positivity. This can help model to children how to face challenges and uncertainties now and into the future.

By focusing on curiosity, kindness and respect, we can instil in children strong values about the need to keep learning and thinking about ourselves and others. These might just be the values and approaches to life that will help children get up each morning with hopefulness about the day ahead and their capacity to deal with it – and ultimately to be hopeful even during the most challenging times.

Activities and resources

There are different types of play for primary school-aged children:

- **Free, unstructured play** – when play just happens and the child uses their imagination and controls the play. This includes creative play alone or with others, including games; imaginative games such as making cubby houses with blankets or dressing up; and exploring spaces like cupboards, backyards, parks and playgrounds. Children may like you to join in their play or not. You can certainly provide them with materials such as dress-ups and gently prompt them to try new things.
- **Structured play** – when play is organised and happens at a fixed time or in a set space. This play is often organised and led by an adult. Examples include family board-games or card games, formal classes to teach swimming, dancing or drama, storytelling sessions, and sports teams.

One way to understand the parents' role in children's play is the Montessori approach where the adult is a "guide". The guide observes the child, sets up the environment to meet their needs, helps connect the child to it, and makes adjustments as needed. This is very much the approach I take when working with children in sessions. This approach can also be used at home to help children feel involved, become independent and responsible, and learn how to contribute to their family and community. Importantly, this approach can also help cultivate a love of learning within the child. This approach includes the role of the parent as guide:

- Preparing a safe physical and psychological environment
- Developing agreements together with the child
- Observing the child and seeking to understand their needs
- Fostering independence and responsibility
- Sparking the child's wonder in the world around them
- Nurturing connection
- Building trust
- Modelling for them
- Cultivating slowness
- Respecting the child, loving them and accepting them
- Helping them become a member of the family and society (Davies & Uzodike, 2024).

Observing your child

- **Interests** – what do they talk about? What activities are they drawn to?
- **Movements** – what movements are they mastering? How do they hold their pencil, climb, swing on monkey bars?
- **Activities they choose** – how long do they work on each activity? How much of the activity do they do? What do they do with the materials? Have they mastered the activity?
- **Where they use the activity** – how do they retrieve the activity? How do they carry it? Do they return it when finished?
- **Independence** – do they choose activities independently? What aids their independence? Are there any obstacles (including ourselves) to independence? How do they ask for help? Do they accept help?

- **Focus** – look for moments when they are deeply focused as well as when they are distracted by someone or something but still able to come back to the activity. Note when their breathing is smooth, when they are regulated, when they look satisfied at completion.
- **Concentration** – what breaks their concentration? Where do they concentrate best? How do you support their concentration (mostly this is by not interrupting, though at times you can step in to help a little, then step back again to let them get further)?
- **Repetition** – do they repeat an activity? If they repeat it, do they do it in the same way or with variety? (Davies & Uzodike, 2024)

Types of play activities

Play activities that you can organise for your child include:

- "I spy"
- Home-made obstacle courses
- Simple cooking and food preparation activities
- Card games and board-games
- Projects that children can work on over time.

Materials you can provide for your child to play with in an unstructured way include:

- Boxes, linen and washing baskets for building cubby houses
- Cut-off pieces of interesting fabric for imaginative play
- Animal play sets – farms, zoos, dinosaurs
- Doll houses with people and furniture.

Benefits of play

Here's a list of the benefits of play for children's development:

- Physical exercise
- Learning and practising communication in a variety of situations

- Mathematical skills
- Expressing emotions
- Interacting with and learning about others
- Making sense of new or challenging situations
- Trying out new things
- Taking risks in a safe environment
- Learning about capacity and boundaries
- Self-discovery.

Activities to help children's social and emotional development

- Think about times when you have felt pleased with your day. Choose a feeling word to capture your experience and share this with your child. This modelling helps children learn how to express feelings. You could add to this by also sharing feelings of upset or annoyance when you experience them, with reasons for why you are feeling that way and what you are going to do when you next feel that way.
- Draw pictures of feelings on faces and bodies. You could google some examples or simply begin with some feelings that your child suggests. You could begin with simple language such as "glad", "sad" and "mad" with younger children and build from there to add nuance and complexity with older children.
- Play a game of charades where each person acts out a feeling and others guess the feeling.
- Use picture books to explore feelings and situations that characters face. Children engage best with books that tell a story and show characters working out what to do rather than books that are too directive or prescriptive and tell children what they should do. Books can help children explore topics that are bothering them without it being too direct or confronting. Giving this space and distance can help children see that they

are not the only ones facing these difficulties and also be more comfortable about then talking about their own worries.

- Create a riddle by making up clues based on your child's interests and spelling ability, then read out the riddle and have the child fill in the blanks. After you've done a few of these, they'll want to make up some for you. For example, baby animals: "My mum has a pouch and strong back legs. We live in the bush. We eat plants. I am a baby kangaroo, called a J _ E _."
- Paper bag puppets: a small paper bag fits nicely over a child's hand. The flap at the bottom is a natural mouth. Paint or glue on lips, teeth, a tongue, then add hair and facial features.
- Continuation storytelling: this is a game of collective storytelling, played in a circle. One person is designated timekeeper, and their job is to stop every player at the end of two minutes. The first player begins to tell a story. At the end of two minutes, the next person has to take up the story where the first player left off, but they can change topics once started. The game is over after the story has been embellished by every player. You could record the stories and play them back later.
- Growing sprouts: your child can grow their own bean, alfalfa or radish sprouts in just a few days. Buy seeds meant for sprouting and eating to avoid chemicals. Soak about half a cup of the seeds overnight in cool water, and rinse them off in the morning. Place the seeds in a large glass jar and cover it with a piece of thin cloth. Secure the cloth with an elastic band. Store the seeds in a dark place, like a kitchen cupboard. Twice a day, rinse the seeds with cool water and drain.

Books for learning about feelings

Suggested books about feelings and worries for reading with children:

- *The Huge Bag of Worries*, Virginia Ironside
- *Hey Warrior: A Book for Kids about Anxiety*, Karen Young

- *How Big Are Your Worries Little Bear?* Jayneen Sanders
- *The Red Tree*, Shaun Tan
- *The Invisible String*, Patrice Karst
- *Brain Is (Not) Always Right*, Scott Stuart

Resources for parents

If you are interested in learning more about children's mental health and difficulties, you will find a lot of useful information at https://raisingchildren.net.au.

If you are concerned about your child's development or mental health, you can talk to your child's teacher and general practitioner as starting points.

For further information about feelings, including understanding your own, these resources will be helpful:

- *The A to Z of Feelings* by Andrew Fuller
- *Atlas of the Heart* by Brené Brown

There are many books about parenting that are readily accessible. Here are some you might like:

- *Little People, Big Feelings* by Gen Muir
- *Brain-Body Parenting* by Mona Delahooke
- *The Parenting Revolution* by Justin Coulson
- *No-Drama Discipline* by Daniel J. Siegel
- *Parental as Anything* by Maggie Dent
- *Raising a Secure Child* by Kent Hoffman and others

Programs for parents

Parenting programs, either in person or online, can also be helpful for parents to learn skills and gain a sense of perspective about how other parents are feeling. There are a range of different programs available with approaches that vary, so it's worth exploring these to see what would be a good fit for you. Some general parenting programs include:

- Tuning in to Kids – https://tuningintokids.org.au/parents/
- Triple P Parenting – https://www.triplep-parenting.net.nz/
- 123 Magic – https://www.123magic.com/
- Parentworks – https://www.parentworks.org.au/
- Parent Effectiveness Training – https://www.gordontraining.com/parent-programs/parent-effectiveness-training-p-e-t/

There are also programs tailored to particular needs, such as parenting after separation and parenting children with Autism Spectrum Disorder. You can contact your local council or organisations such as Relationships Australia to find out what's available in your local area.

References

Australian Bureau of Statistics. (2022). *Marriages and divorces, Australia.* https://www.abs.gov.au/statistics/people/people-and-communities/marriages-and-divorces-australia/latest-release

Australian Institute for Disaster Resilience. (2020). *Our world our say: National survey of children and young people on climate change and disaster risk.* https://resourcecentre.savethechildren.net/document/our-world-our-say-national-survey-children-and-young-people-climate-change-and-disaster-risk/

Brackett, M. (2019). *Permission to feel: Unlocking the power of emotions to achieve wellbeing and success.* Quercus Books.

Charles, C., & Louv, R. (2020). Wild hope: The transformative power of children engaging with nature. In A. Cutter-Mackenzie-Knowles, K. Malone, & E. Barratt Hacking (Eds.), *Research handbook on childhoodnature.* Springer International Handbooks of Education. Springer.

Davies, S., & Uzodike, J. (2024). *The Montessori child: A parent's guide to raising capable children with creative minds and compassionate hearts.* Workman Publishing.

DelGiudice, M. (2018). Middle childhood: An evolutionary-developmental synthesis. In N. Halfon, C. B. Forrest, R. M. Lerner, & E. M. Faustman (Eds.), *Handbook of life course health development.* Springer.

Durlak, J. A., Mahoney, J. L., & Boyle, A. E. (2022). What we know and what we need to find out about universal, school-based social and emotional learning programs for children and adolescents: A review of meta-analyses and directions for future research. *Psychological Bulletin, 148*(11–12), 765–82.

Edwards, S. L. (2017). Reflecting differently. New dimensions: reflection-before-action and reflection-beyond-action. *International Practice Development Journal, 7*(1), 1–14.

Faber, A., & Mazlish, E. (2012). *How to talk so kids will listen and listen so kids will talk.* Bonnier Books.

Flood, M., Adams, K., & Crabbe, M. (2024). By the time they are 20, more than 4 in 5 men and 2 in 3 women have been exposed to pornography: new research. *The Conversation.*

Frydenberg, E. (2022). *Coping in good times and bad: Developing fortitude.* Melbourne University Publishing.

Hamilton, V. (2023). *Talking sex: A conversation guide for parents.* Amba Press.

Hawthorne, B., & Yglesias, N. (2022). *Raising antiracist children: A practical parenting guide.* Simon Element.

Hudson, J. L., Minihan, S., Chen, W., Carl, T., Fu, M., Tully, L., Kangas, M., Rosewell, L., McDermott, E. A., Wang, Y., Stubbs, T., & Martiniuk, A. (2023). Interventions for young children's mental health: A review of reviews. *Clinical Child and Family Psychology Review, 26*(3), 593–641.

Kanojia, A. (2024). *How to raise a healthy gamer.* Bluebird.

Kennedy-Moore, E. (2012). Children's growing friendships: How children's understanding of friendship changes and develops with age. *Psychology Today.* https://www.psychologytoday.com/us/blog/growing-friendships/201202/childrens-growing-friendships

Koukourikos, K., Tsaloglidou, A., Tzeha, L., Iliadis, C., Frantzana, A., Katsimbeli, A., & Kourkouta, L. (2021). An overview of play therapy. *Materia Sociomedica, 33*(4), 293–97.

Lawson, D. F., Stevenson, K. T., Peterson, M. N., et al. (2019). Children can foster climate change concern among their parents. *Nature Climate Change, 9,* 458–62.

Martin, E. (1992). *Children at play: Creative games and activities for six to nine-year olds.* Millennium Books.

Mitchell, M. (2023). *Tweens: What kids need now, before the teenage years.* Penguin Random House.

National Mental Health Commission. (2021). *National Children's Mental Health and Wellbeing Strategy.*

Neff, K. (2021). *Self-compassion: The proven power of being kind to yourself.* Yellow Kite.

Prilleltensky, I., & Prilleltensky, O. (2021). *How people matter: Why it affects health, happiness, love, work, and society.* Cambridge University Press.

Rosenthal, R., & Jacobsen, L. (1966). Teachers' expectations: Determinants of pupils' IQ gains. *Psychological Reports, 19,* 115–18.

Royal Children's Hospital National Child Health Poll, The. (2020). *COVID-19 pandemic: Effects on the lives of Australian children and families. Poll Number 18.* The Royal Children's Hospital Melbourne, Parkville. Victoria.

Salamon, M. (2024). *Co-regulation: Helping children and teens navigate big emotions.* Harvard Health Publishing.

Salmivalli, C., Kaudiainen, A., Kaistaniemi, L., & Lagerspetz, K. M. J. (1999). Self-evaluated self-esteem, peer-evaluated self-esteem, and defensive egotism as predictors of adolescents' participation in bullying situations. *Personality and Social Psychology Bulletin, 25*(10), 1268–78.

Sanson, A., & Bellemo, M. (2021). Children and youth in the climate crisis. *BJPsych Bulletin, 45*(4), 205–9.

Sanson, A. V., Malca, K. V. P., Van Hoorn, J. L., & Burke, S. E. L. (2022). *Children and climate change.* Cambridge University Press.

School of Life, The. (2023). *Reasons to be hopeful: What remains consoling, inspiring and beautiful.* The School of Life.

Snyder, C. R., Rand, K. L., & Sigmon, D. R. (2002). Hope theory: A member of the positive psychology family. In C. R. Snyder & S. J. Lopez (Eds.), *The handbook of positive psychology* (pp. 257–76). Oxford University Press.

Solnit, R. (2016). *Hope in the dark: Untold histories, wild possibilities.* Canongate Books Ltd.

Stewart, R. (2023). *Creating connections: Inspire your child to thrive in their learning.* Amba Press.

Turnbull, D. (2021). *50 Risks to take with your kids: A guide to building resilience and independence in the first 10 years.* Hardie Grant.

University of Melbourne. (2018). Eight and nine-year-olds experience poor body image as hormone levels rise. *Science Daily.* https://www.sciencedaily.com/releases/2018/08/180814101515.htm

World Health Organisation. (2023). *Improving the mental and brain health of children and adolescents.* https://www.who.int/activities/improving-the-mental-and-brain-health-of-children-and-adolescents

Yalom, I. (1980). *Existential psychotherapy.* Basic Books.

Acknowledgements

There are many people to thank for bringing this book to fruition – the physical existence of the book relies on the commitment of the publishing team, Alicia, Andrew and Tess, to not only appreciate its value but make it the best it can be. My drive for writing a book about hope for parents comes from the work I do as a psychologist, seeing the efforts of parents and carers in supporting their children when life gets difficult. The encouragement of colleagues, some of whom provided feedback on an earlier draft, was appreciated in validating the importance of the work. My family, particularly my daughters, Laura and Caitlin, continue to support my work and help me to keep reflecting on what parenting means across the lifespan. Now having a granddaughter, Kleo, makes this work more important than ever.

www.ingramcontent.com/pod-product-compliance
Lightning Source LLC
Chambersburg PA
CBHW050414120526
44590CB00015B/1965